THE PIANIST & TAKING SIDES

Ronald Harwood's plays include *The Dresser*, *Another Time*, *Taking Sides*, *Quartet*, and *Mahler's Conversion*. He is also author of *Sir Donald Wolfit, CBE: His Life and Work in the Unfashionable Theatre*, and a history of theatre, *All the World's a Stage*. He is the editor of *The Faber Book of Theatre*. He was Visitor in Theatre at Balliol College, Oxford, was President of English PEN from 1990 to 1993, and President of International PEN from 1993 to 1997. In 2000 he was awarded the Stefan Mitrov Ljubisa Prize for his contribution to European Literature and Human Rights. He was elected Chairman of the Royal Society for Literature in 2001. In 1996 he was appointed Chevalier de l'Ordre des Arts et des Lettres, and in 1999 he was awarded a CBE. He was made Hon. Doctor of Letters by Keele University in 2002.

THE PIANIST
&
TAKING SIDES

Ronald Harwood

ff

faber and faber

First published in 2002
by Faber and Faber Limited
3 Queen Square London WCIN 3AU
Published in the United States by Faber and Faber Inc.
an affiliate of Farrar, Straus and Giroux LLC, New York

Typeset by Country Setting, Kingsdown, Kent CT14 8ES
Printed in England by Mackays of Chatham plc, Chatham, Kent

A CIP record for this book
is available from the British Library

ISBN 0-571-21281-6

2 4 6 8 10 9 7 5 3 1

CONTENTS

The Pianist

The Pianist

based on the published memoir by
Wladyslaw Szpilman

CAST AND CREW

MAIN CAST

WLADYSLAW SZPILMAN	Adrien Brody
MAJOREK	Daniel Caltagirone
CAPT. WILM HOSENFELD	Thomas Kretschman
THE FATHER	Frank Finlay
THE MOTHER	Maureen Lipman
DOROTA	Emilia Fox
HENRYK	Ed Stoppard
REGINA	Julia Rayner
HALINA	Jessica Kate Meyer
JANINA	Ruth Platt
KITTIE	Katarzyna Figura
POLISH WOMAN	Nina Franoszek
MICHAL	Valentine Pelka
RUBENSTEIN	Popeck
BOGUCKI	Ronan Vibert
CUSTOMER WITH COINS	Zbigniew Zamachowski
GERMAN SOLDIER	Joachim Paul Assböck
POLISH OFFICER	John Keogh
GERMAN SOLDIER	Thomas Lawincky
GERMAN OFFICER	Wanja Mues

MAIN CREW

Director	Roman Polanski
Screenplay	Ronald Harwood
Producers	Robert Benmussa, Roman Polanski, Alain Sarde
Co-Producer	Gene Gutowski
Executive Producers	Timothy Burrill, Henning Molfenter, Lew Rywin
Associate Producer	Rainer Schaper
Cinematography	Pawel Edelman
Music	Wojciech Kilar
Costume	Anna B. Sheppard
Editor	Hervè de Luze
Production Design	Sebastian T. Krawinkel

Note

Unless otherwise indicated, all dialogue spoken by
Germans will be in the German language and subtitled.

Fade in:

INT. WARSAW (ARCHIVE) — DAY

Black and white. Street scene. People toing and froing. A tram rattles by.

Superimpose caption:

WARSAW 1939

INT. STUDIO, RADIO STATION, WARSAW — DAY

Wladyslav Szpilman plays Chopin's Nocturne in C sharp minor, Posthumous. He's twenty-eight years old, elegant and handsome.

In the booth, separated from the studio by a glass screen, an engineer, wearing collar and tie, monitors the broadcast. Behind him, a window to the street with strips of paper taped on it as protection against blast.

Without warning, a bomb drops nearby, then another and another. The whole building shudders alarmingly and the window in the booth shatters.

The engineer and Szpilman exchange a look as a man enters the booth and talks urgently to the Engineer, then goes.

The engineer makes a 'cut-throat' gesture, but Szpilman shakes his head, determined to play on.

He plays, then glances at the booth. The engineer has gone, but through the shattered window he sees fires raging.

Very near, a loud, terrifying explosion. The reverberations cause plaster to flake and dust to trickle down over his face.

And then a bomb explodes even closer. The glass screen separating booth from studio implodes, showering Szpilman with glass. He stops, frozen.

INT. STAIRS AND LOBBY, RADIO STATION — DAY

Pandemonium. Chaos. People rushing in all directions, many carrying files, boxes, papers, shouting, calling. Some of the men in military uniform. The bombing continuous.

Szpilman fights his way down the stairs. He has a small cut on his forehead and is dabbing it with his handkerchief. He has a dazed look.

Halfway down the stairs, a young woman, Dorota, tugs at his sleeve:

> DOROTA
>
> Mr Szpilman —

He turns, to see an extremely pretty young woman gazing adoringly at him while they're jostled and shoved. His eyes light up.

> SZPILMAN
>
> Hello —

> DOROTA
>
> I came specially to meet you today. I love your playing, but what a day to choose —

> SZPILMAN
>
> Who are you?

> DOROTA
>
> My name's Dorota, I'm Jurek's sister — oh! you're bleeding.

> SZPILMAN
>
> It's nothing —

Jurek pushes in beside them and takes her arm.

> JUREK
>
> C'mon, Dorota, you can write him a fan letter later, this isn't the best time, c'mon —

Jurek, pulling Dorota, fights his way down the stairs.

> SZPILMAN
> (calling)
> Jurek, why have you been hiding her?

And he, too, is carried with the flow into the lobby.

Debris everywhere. Szpilman fights to get to the main door, when another bomb explodes, filling the air with dust and debris, obscuring him and everyone else.

INT. WARSAW APARTMENT — DUSK

The Szpilman family in panic: coming and going out of rooms, packing clothes and belongings into open suitcases and a trunk in a comfortable, tastefully furnished bourgeois apartment, the living room lined with books, paintings and boasting a boudoir grand, silver platters and candlesticks.

The family consist of Mother, in a state of great anxiety, Father, Regina, twenty-six, Halina, twenty-two, and Henryk, twenty-four, the only one not in movement. He sits by the radio set, ear to the speaker, trying to tune to a station.

No bombs now, just the distant sound of artillery fire.

Father, holding a silver-framed photograph, crosses to Mother.

> FATHER
> What you think, should I take Uncle Szymon's photograph?

> MOTHER
> Take it, don't take it, take what you like. Can't you see I'm worried sick?

> FATHER
> He'll come home, he'll be all right –

He goes into his room. She can barely control her tears and hurries into the kitchen just as the front door opens and Szpilman enters, looks round bemused by the activity.

> REGINA
> Mama, Wladek's home –

Mother dashes out of the kitchen.

> MOTHER
> Thank God – Wladek! You're wounded –

7

SZPILMAN

It's a little cut, nothing –

MOTHER

I've been worried sick –

HENRYK

I told her not to worry. You had your papers on you. If you'd
been hit by a bomb, they'd have known where to take you –

The girls suppress smiles.

MOTHER

Henryk, don't say things like that, God forbid, God forbid –

HALINA
(*calling through a door*)
Papa, Wladek's home –

Father appears in the doorway, beaming, clutching a violin case.

FATHER

What did I tell you?

SZPILMAN
(*looking around the room, bemused*)
What are you doing?

REGINA

What's it look like we're doing?

The toing and froing continues non-stop.

SZPILMAN
(*to Henryk*)
They bombed us, we're off the air.

HENRYK

Warsaw's not the only radio station –

MOTHER

Pack, darling, get your things, pack –

SZPILMAN

Where are we going?

8

MOTHER

Out of Warsaw –

SZPILMAN

Out of Warsaw. Where?

REGINA

You haven't heard?

SZPILMAN

Heard what?

REGINA

Haven't you seen the paper? Where's the paper?

She starts to look. The others continue to bustle and pack.

HALINA

I used it for packing.

REGINA
(*exasperated*)

She used it for packing –

FATHER

The government's moved to Lublin.

HALINA

All able-bodied men must leave the city, go across the river
and set up a new line of defence, that's what it said –

FATHER

There's hardly anybody left in this building, only women,
the men have gone –

SZPILMAN

And what do you think you'll do while you're setting up a
new line of defence? Wander round lugging your suitcases?

MOTHER

Pack, Wladek, there's no time –

SZPILMAN

I'm not going anywhere.

HALINA

Good! I'm not going anywhere either!

MOTHER

Don't be ridiculous, we've got to keep together –

SZPILMAN

No, no, no, I'm staying put. If I'm going to die, I prefer to die at home.

MOTHER

God forbid –

HENRYK

Sssh!

Crackles, whistles and static from the radio.

Ssh! I've got something, listen –

They gather round.

RADIO ANNOUNCER

– an important announcement. News has just been received through the BBC that Great Britain, having had no reply – (*static*) – and therefore has declared war on Nazi Germany – (*a collective gasp*) – next few hours – awaiting latest news –

Henryk hits the set.

– but France is expected to make a similar announcement – (*static*) – Poland is no longer alone.

The Polish national anthem plays. All are still.

INT. WARSAW APARTMENT – NIGHT

Father pours liqueur into glasses.

The family are seated around the dining table, having just finished a meal. The table groans with the remains of the dinner. Szpilman has a plaster over his cut.

HENRYK
(*lighting up a cigarette*)
Mama, that was a great dinner.

SZPILMAN

It certainly was.

MOTHER

When there's something to celebrate, you've got to make an effort.

The glasses are handed round.

FATHER

Here's to Great Britain and France.

They all clink glasses and drink.

I told you. Didn't I tell you? All will be well –

EXT. RUINED WARSAW STREET – DAY

A column of German soldiers, led by an officer on horseback, march into view.

On the sidewalk of the street, with its buildings in ruins, smoke still rising, stand onlookers, including Szpilman and Henryk, and a little behind them, Father, craning to see.

They watch, expressionless, as the Germans march past.

INT. WARSAW APARTMENT – DAY

Regina is opening and closing the window, examining the frame with her fingers. Halina is on a box, removing and replacing books. Mother sits at one end of the table, polishing a man's watch and chain. At the other end, Father sits counting a small stack of notes and coins. Henryk is deep in thought and Szpilman is fiddling with his father's violin.

The apartment has less furniture now and the silver has gone.

FATHER
(*finishing the counting*)

Five thousand and three.

MOTHER

Is that all?

FATHER

Yes, five thousand and three zlotys, that's all we've got left.

REGINA

It's three thousand and three zlotys too much. (*reading from newspaper*) 'Re: Further restrictions regarding liquid assets: Jews will be allowed to keep a maximum of two thousand zlotys in their homes.'

MOTHER

What are we supposed to do with the rest?

HALINA

Deposit it in a bank. Blocked account –

HENRYK

Banks? Who'd be stupid enough to deposit money in a German bank?

REGINA

We could hide the money here in the window frame –

FATHER

No, no, no. I'll tell you what we'll do. We'll use tried and tested methods. You know what we did in the last war? We made a hole in the table leg and we hid the money in there.

HENRYK

And suppose they take the table away?

MOTHER

What d'you mean, take the table away?

HENRYK

The Germans go into Jewish homes and they just take what they want, furniture, valuables, anything –

MOTHER

Do they?

FATHER

Idiot! What would they want with a table?

All look at the table: it's covered in stains and the veneer is coming away at one end.

A table like this?

He pokes his finger under the veneer. It snaps, revealing bare wood beneath.

MOTHER

What on earth are you doing?

HALINA

There's a good place under the cupboard.

HENRYK

No, no. Listen, I've been thinking –

SZPILMAN

That makes a change –

HENRYK

You know what we do? We use psychology.

SZPILMAN

We use what?

HENRYK

We leave the money and the watch on the table. And we cover it like this (*Covers it with the newspaper.*) In full view. The Germans will search high and low, I promise you, they'll never notice it –

SZPILMAN

Of course they'll notice it. But look – (*Lifts the violin finger-board.*) – this is a good place for something.

HENRYK

A good place for what? (*to the others*) He's insane!

SZPILMAN

Just shut up –

FATHER
(*overlapping*)

My violin?

They all talk at once.

REGINA

Quiet! Quiet! Order, please, order!

                    HALINA
She's a lawyer, she likes order –

                    REGINA
Listen, just listen. Let's come to an agreement. We jam the
money in the window frame. The watch we hide under the
cupboard. And the chain we put in the violin.

A brief silence.

                    FATHER
Will I still be able to play?

                    SZPILMAN
Let's find out –

They start to hide the things.

INT. WARSAW PHARMACY – DAY

*Szpilman is on the public telephone, waiting for someone to answer
his call. Then:*

                    SZPILMAN
Jurek? Wladek Szpilman.

                    JUREK
                  (*filtered*)
Wladek! How are you?

                    SZPILMAN
Fine, we're fine, thank you, and you?

                    JUREK
                  (*filtered*)
Fine, we're fine in the circumstances. But I can guess what
you've called about. There's nothing we can do; they won't
reopen the station –

                    SZPILMAN
              (*trying to interrupt*)
Yes, I know, but Jurek, Jurek –

JUREK
(*filtered*)

– not even music, nothing, no radios for the Poles. But I'm
sure you'll find work, Wladek, a pianist like you.

SZPILMAN

Maybe, maybe not, but, Jurek, don't be offended, I didn't
call to discuss my future career –

EXT. WARSAW STREET AND CAFÉ PARADISO – DAY

*Szpilman and Dorota stroll along a tree-lined street with bombed-out
buildings and rubble.*

*She flicks admiring, almost loving glances at him as they walk and
talk. And he is smiling, touched by her.*

DOROTA

I nagged Jurek for weeks and weeks. And at last he gave
in and said, 'All right, come with me tomorrow,' and so
I came and they bombed the station.

SZPILMAN

You know something? Meeting you like that was absolutely
wonderful.

DOROTA

Really?

SZPILMAN

Yes! (*He looks at her, smiles.*) It was – it was unforgettable.

She's embarrassed.

DOROTA

I've always loved your playing, Mr Szpilman –

SZPILMAN

Wladek, please –

DOROTA

No one plays Chopin like you.

SZPILMAN

I hope that's a compliment.

DOROTA

Of course! I mean it, I mean it!

SZPILMAN

I know, I was just making a little joke. Shall we go to the
Paradiso, have a coffee?

DOROTA

I'd like that –

They walk on.

SZPILMAN

And you. What do you do?

DOROTA

I finished at the conservatoire –

SZPILMAN

You're a musician?

DOROTA

Yes – well – but only just –

SZPILMAN

What instrument?

DOROTA

The cello.

SZPILMAN

The cello! I love to see a woman playing the cello. Here
we are –

They have come to the café but stop dead.

'Café Paradiso' on the door, and in a window the sign:

NO JEWS

They stand and stare in silence. Then:

DOROTA

But – but this is monstrous! How dare they! It's disgraceful –

SZPILMAN

Yes, but you know what people are like. They want to be better Nazis than Hitler –

DOROTA

I'm going in there to complain –

SZPILMAN

Don't, don't, Dorota, it's better not, believe me –

DOROTA

It's so humiliating. Someone like you –

SZPILMAN

Maybe we can find somewhere else –

DOROTA

We could walk in the park –

SZPILMAN

No. We can't. Now that's an official decree. No Jews allowed in the park.

DOROTA

Oh my God, are you joking?

SZPILMAN

No, I'm not joking. It's true, believe me. I'd suggest we just sit on a bench somewhere, but that's another official decree, Jews are not allowed to sit on public benches.

DOROTA

But this is – this is – totally absurd!

SZPILMAN

I'll tell you what we can do. We can just stand here and talk. I think we're allowed to do that, don't you?

A mock conversation:

So, you play the cello, Dorota, that's nice, and who's your favourite composer? Really? Chopin? Well, you'll have to play his Cello Sonata, won't you? And what about you, Wladek?

She begins to laugh.

I could accompany you, me on the piano, you on the cello –

They become almost helpless, holding on to each other.

> DOROTA
> Oh, Mr Szpilman, you're quite – quite wonderful –

> SZPILMAN
> Wladek, please –

Amidst their laughter, he takes her hand and kisses it.

INT. WARSAW APARTMENT – NIGHT

The family are gathered around the table, listening to Father reading from the newspaper.

The apartment has even less furniture now. The paintings are gone.

> FATHER
> (*reading*)
> 'Re: emblems for Jews in the Warsaw District. I hereby order that all Jews in the Warsaw District will wear visible emblems when out of doors. This decree will come into force on the 1st December 1939 and applies to all Jews over twelve years of age. The emblem will be worn on the right sleeve and will represent a blue Star of David on a white background. The background must be sufficiently large for the Star to measure eight centimetres from point to point. The width of the arms of the Star must be one centimetre. Jews who do not respect this decree will be severely punished. Governor of Warsaw District, Dr Fischer.'

Silence. Then:

> HENRYK
> I won't wear it.

> REGINA
> I won't wear it. I'm not going to be branded –

SZPILMAN
(*grabbing the newspaper*)

Let me see this –

FATHER

Doesn't it say we have to provide these armbands ourselves? Where will we get them?

HENRYK

We're not going to get them. We're not going to wear them!

Silence, each locked in their own thoughts.

EXT. WARSAW STREET – DAY

Father, wearing the Star of David armband, walks slowly along, carrying a string bag containing potatoes and carrots, his eyes fixed on the pavement as if his thoughts are a million miles away.

He passes two German officers. They stop.

I GERMAN OFFICER
(*a harsh shout*)

You!

Father stops, turns fearfully and approaches the Germans.

I GERMAN OFFICER

Why didn't you bow?

FATHER
(*removing his hat*)

I'm sorry I –

I German Officer cracks him hard across the face, catching his ear. Father reels, collects himself as best he can and starts to shuffle on –

I GERMAN OFFICER
(*calling after him*)

You are forbidden to walk on the pavement. Walk in the gutter!

Father steps off the pavement and walks in the gutter. The German officers turn and go. Father walks on.

INT. WARSAW APARTMENT — EVENING

Szpilman composing at the piano. He plays, makes adjustments with a pencil to the manuscript, plays again.

The flat is almost bare.

Halina, enters with a newspaper.

> HALINA
>
> Have you seen this?

> SZPILMAN
> (*irritated*)
> What, I'm working, what?

She hands him the paper. He looks at it. His expression darkens.

Insert – the newspaper. A map of the proposed Jewish area: two distinct districts, one large, one smaller.

> SZPILMAN'S VOICE
>
> What is it?

> HALINA'S VOICE
>
> That's where they're going to put us.

> SZPILMAN'S VOICE
>
> What d'you mean, put us?

The apartment:

She looks over his shoulder and reads. As she does so, the door of Henryk's room opens and he stands leaning in the doorway, watching, as if amused.

> HALINA
>
> 'By order of the Governor of the Warsaw District, Dr Fischer, concerning the establishment of the Jewish District in Warsaw. There will be created a Jewish District in which all Jews living in Warsaw or moving to Warsaw will have to reside.' And look here: 'Jews living outside of the prescribed area will have to move to the Jewish district by 31st of October 1940.'

Szpilman gazes at the map, horrified.

SZPILMAN

But – they won't get all of us – we'll – it's too small – there's four hundred thousand of us in Warsaw!

HENRYK

No. Three hundred and sixty thousand, so it'll be easy –

He laughs but they're disturbed by a sound from another room, the sound of crying. They look at each other puzzled, then Halina opens a door and looks in. Szpilman and Henryk join her.

Bedroom:

Father is asleep but Mother is sitting on the bed, holding a purse, crying. Halina sits beside her, puts an arm round her.

HALINA

Mama, what is it?

Mother opens the purse to reveal a crumpled note.

MOTHER

Twenty zlotys. That's all we've got left. What can I buy with twenty zlotys? (*breaking down*) I'm sick of cooking potatoes, potatoes, potatoes –

She weeps. Halina tries to comfort her. Szpilman and Henryk watch.

INT. SZPILMAN APARTMENT, SLISKA STREET — NIGHT

Hands on the piano keyboard. Podgy, hairy hands with dirty nails. They play an octave, harsh, toneless, with straight fingers.

The hands belong to Mr Lipa, a dealer, early fifties. He sits at the piano, now examining the lacquer. Regina stands in the bow, watching him. Henryk is at the table, also watching intently.

Szpilman sits apart, aloof, his back to the piano and to Mr Lipa.

MR LIPA

That's the price. That's what I'm offering. And my advice is to accept. You won't get more from anyone else.

REGINA

But – but it's a Steinway, Mr Lipa –

21

MR LIPA

Two thousand. My advice is to take it. What you going to
do when you're hungry? Eat the piano?

*Henryk suddenly makes a lunge for him, grabs hold of him, a rough
struggle takes place and during it Mother and Father appear at their
bedroom door to watch, appalled.*

HENRYK

Get out! You're a thieving bastard, we don't want your
money, get out! We'd rather give it away! Get out!

Regina tries physically to restrain him.

MR LIPA
(overlapping, warding off Henryk)

Hey! Hey! What's the matter with you? Haven't you eaten
today, what you suffering from? Hey!

REGINA
(overlapping)

Henryk, stop it, leave him alone –

MR LIPA
(recovering, catching his breath, overlapping)

You people are crazy! I'm doing you a favour, two thousand,
and I'm paying for the removal, I'm not even charging for
the removal –

Henryk subsides, glowering at him.

You haven't eaten today, you're crazy –

Suddenly:

SZPILMAN
(turning to them, severe)

Take it.

EXT. STREET LEADING TO GHETTO — DAY

*Autumn. A great column of Jews of all ages make their way towards
the area that will become the ghetto. On foot, on bicycles, on horse-
drawn platforms, some pushing prams loaded with belongings. A great
moving mass of humanity.*

They're watched on either side of the street by Poles.

On a horse-drawn platform, the Szpilmans with their belongings. All wear armbands.

Szpilman, Halina and Henryk walk beside the platform with Mother, Father and Regina seated on it.

Szpilman catches sight of someone among the onlookers, smiles and pushes through the crowd to Dorota, close to tears.

SZPILMAN

Dorota!

DOROTA

I didn't want to come, I didn't want to see all this, but I couldn't stop myself.

SZPILMAN

How are you doing?

DOROTA

Fine, no, not really, they arrested my cousin, but Jurek says they'll let him out – (*Stops, tears in her eyes.*) This is disgraceful –

SZPILMAN

Don't worry, it won't last long –

DOROTA

That's what I said, it's so – it's too absurd!

SZPILMAN

I'll see you – soon –

He smiles and runs to catch up with his family. He looks back, but Dorota is lost to sight and the procession continues on its way.

INT./EXT. GHETTO APARTMENT AND STREET — DAY

Two rooms on the third floor: a living room and a kitchen. The Szpilmans are unpacking their belongings in silence. Father pauses for a moment to take stock.

FATHER

To tell you the truth, I thought it would be worse.

SZPILMAN

How will we sleep?

MOTHER

I'll sleep with the girls in the kitchen. You, Henryk and Papa in here.

HALINA
(*at a window*)
Look! Come and look –

They all go to the window and look out.

Their point of view – the street.

Further along, men are building a wall across the street.

EXT. GHETTO WALL – DAY

A series of shots:

The wall. The wall. The wall.

EXT. MARKET AREA, GHETTO – DAY

Winter. Cold, freezing day. Slush underfoot. Great activity. People selling shoes, clothes, carpets, curtains, food. A woman offers cakes under a barbed-wire cover. Noise, bustle, restless toing and froing.

Among the traders, Henryk, slightly shabbier now, and at his feet a basket with books. He holds a couple of volumes in his hands, trying to interest passers-by.

Szpilman, also a little shabbier, wends his way through the sellers and buyers, the beggars, the passers-by, and reaches Henryk.

Henryk drops the two volumes into the basket, takes a handle one side of the basket, Szpilman the other. They set off.

As they walk, carrying the basket between them, passing beggars and children asking for food:

SZPILMAN

You sell anything?

HENRYK

Just one. Dostoevsky. *The Idiot.* Three zlotys.

SZPILMAN

That's better than yesterday.

HENRYK

Three lousy zlotys. And there are people here making
millions –

SZPILMAN

I know –

HENRYK

You don't know, believe me. They bribe the guards. The
guards turn a blind eye. They're bringing in cartloads, food,
tobacco, liquor, French cosmetics, and the poor are dying
all around them and they don't give a damn.

*Suddenly, a woman appears in front of them, barring their way. She's
brightly rouged with thickly painted eyebrows, dressed in an old green
velvet curtain with an unsteady mauve ostrich feather rising from her
straw hat.*

THE FEATHER WOMAN

Excuse me, but have you by any chance seen my husband
Izaak Szerman?

SZPILMAN

I'm afraid not –

THE FEATHER WOMAN

A tall handsome man with a little grey beard?

They shake their heads.

No? (*She is near to tears, then smiles artificially.*) Oh, do
forgive me. (*as she goes*) Goodbye, sleep well, if you see
him, please do write, Izaak Szerman's his name –

*She wanders on. Szpilman and Henryk, too, continue on their way.
And as they go:*

25

HENRYK

Sometimes I wish I could go mad.

EXT. CHLODNA STREET — DAY

A stream of cars and trams. Jewish policemen and German soldiers much in evidence.

Szpilman and Henryk join a large crowd of Jews waiting at a barrier to cross the intersection. The crowd is agitated, impatient for a policeman to stop the traffic and let them through.

A man next to Szpilman and Henryk is becoming more and more distraught, shifting his weight from foot to foot, taking off and putting on his hat.

THE NERVOUS MAN

This is totally insane; why do we have to have a gentile street running through our area? Can't they go around?

HENRYK

Don't worry about it, they're about to build a bridge, haven't you heard?

THE NERVOUS MAN

A bridge, a schmidge, and the Germans claim to be intelligent. You know what I think? I think they're totally stupid. I've got a family to feed and I spend half my time here waiting for them to let us through –

Meanwhile, a street band begins to play a waltz. Jewish policemen and German soldiers are clearing a space, shoving Jews out of the way, including Szpilman, Henryk and the nervous man. Other soldiers are clearing a space.

Two German soldiers pull out of the crowd a tall woman and a short man and haul them into the cleared space.

THE GERMAN SOLDIER

Dance!

The couple dance to the street band's waltz.

At intervals, German soldiers select even more unlikely couples: a fat woman with a painfully thin man, a young boy with an elderly woman, two men, and two cripples.

The German soldiers are, to various degrees, amused. One of them is almost hysterical with laughter.

> SOLDIERS
> Faster! Go on, faster! Dance!

The couples dance as fast as they can. A soldier kicks one of the cripples who can't go on any more.

> SOLDIERS
> Dance! Dance!

Then a whistle blows, a policeman stops the traffic, the barrier swings open and people swarm across in both directions.

INT. GHETTO APARTMENT — DAY

Szpilman and Henryk enter and stop. Uneasy.

> MOTHER
> Good, they're here. Yitzchak Heller's been waiting for you, Henryk –

Seated at the table with Mother and Father is a uniformed young man, Yitzchak Heller, unusual appearance, a man with red hair and a Hitler moustache.

Heller remains seated, just nods at the brothers.

> HENRYK
> What's this about?

> MOTHER
> Sit down, have tea, I'll start lunch when the girls get back –

Henryk and Szpilman sit. They eye Heller suspiciously.

> HENRYK
> So, what are you doing here?

FATHER

He brought cakes –

Awkward silence.

His father's back in the jewellery business and doing well, isn't that so, Yitzchak? Amazing. Jewellery –

He runs dry. Another awkward silence. Then:

HELLER

We're recruiting.

HENRYK

Who's recruiting?

HELLER

Don't be clever with me, Henryk. I've come here as a friend. They're bringing Jews in from all over the country. Soon there'll be half a million people in the ghetto. We need more Jewish police –

HENRYK
(*sarcastic*)

Oh? More Jewish police? You mean you want me to wear a cap like yours, beat up Jews with my truncheon and catch the Gestapo spirit. I see!

HELLER
(*eyes narrowed, dangerous*)

Someone's got to do it, Henryk –

HENRYK

But why me? I thought you only recruited boys with rich fathers. Look at my father, look at us, I mean –

HELLER
(*interrupting, flaring*)

Yes, I'm looking at you and that's why I'm here. Your whole family can have a better life. You want to go on struggling for survival, selling books on the street?

HENRYK
(*a smile*)

Yes, please.

HELLER
(*to Szpilman*)

I'm doing you people a favour. And what about you,
Wladek? You're a great pianist. And we've got an excellent
police jazz band. They'd welcome you with open arms. Join
us. You've got no work –

SZPILMAN

Thank you. But I've got work.

Silence. Heller rises angrily.

INT. CAFÉ NOWACZESNA, GHETTO – DAY

*On a platform, Szpilman plays at a piano, but he can hardly be heard
above the noise of chatter and laughter.*

*The large café is crowded, hot and smoke-filled. Well-heeled customers,
pimps, whores, businessmen sit at little tables, eating, talking, laughing,
almost drowning the piano music. Some dance.*

*A couple of tables back from the piano, a customer is doing business
with a friend. The customer has a small stack of coins, some of them
twenty-dollar gold pieces. He folds back the tablecloth to reveal a
marble surface beneath. He drops a coin on the marble and listens but
the noise is too loud. He sees the café owner, Benek, fiftyish, and makes
gestures, pointing at Szpilman.*

Benek pushes his way through to Szpilman.

BENEK
(*whispering into Szpilman's ear*)

I'm sorry, Mr Wladek, he wants you to stop –

SZPILMAN
(*continuing to play*)

Who wants me to stop?

*Benek points to the customer, who makes an imploring gesture to
Szpilman. Szpilman stops playing.*

*The friend watches the customer intently as he drops the coins one by
one onto the marble. He drops them, puts his ear close and listens. Two*

or three he discards, but he smiles when coins make a pure tone, and he keeps them.

Szpilman exchanges looks with a pretty whore, who makes eyes at him.

Satisfied, the customer beams, nods his thanks to Szpilman, who resumes his piano playing.

EXT. GHETTO STREET — DUSK

Szpilman walking. He passes emaciated children and beggars. He steps over the corpses lying on the sidewalk.

EXT. STREET NEAR WALL — DUSK

The wall runs the length of the street, dividing it in half and narrowing it. Buildings on one side, the wall on the other.

Szpilman walks along. A piercing whistle from the Aryan side. Szpilman stops.

Two women appear from a doorway, approach the wall and look up. Two or three packages come flying over from the Aryan side. The women grab them and disappear.

Szpilman walks on and sees a child appear through a hole at ground level. The child wriggles through then turns, pulls a package after him and runs.

Szpilman walks on, hears a noise, looks back to see a second child trying to wriggle through the same hole. But he's stuck. Angry German voices from the Aryan side.

2ND CHILD
Help me – help me –

Szpilman goes to him, pulls him with all his might but the boy is jammed in the hole.

From the other side of the wall, the sound of an angry German voice and of a boot stamping violently on the boy. The boy screams in agony.

Szpilman continues to try to pull the boy through.

The sound of the German voice swearing and the dull, crunching noise made by the boot smashing into the boy continues, and with every thud the boy screams in terrible pain.

Szpilman struggles to help the boy whose screams are becoming weaker yet increasingly desperate.

Szpilman pulls his arms and finally manages to get him through. The boy lies moaning.

Szpilman takes the boy's face in his hands, tries to comfort him, revive him, but the boy has stopped moaning. His head lolls and his jaw sags. He is dead. Szpilman stands quickly and hurries away.

EXT. COURTYARD AND HOUSE — EVENING

Szpilman approaches the house through a shabby yard.

INT. JEHUDA ZYSKIND'S ROOM — EVENING

The noise of a mimeograph machine. A huge, cheerful man with a perpetual cigarette in his mouth.

JEHUDA

I always say look on the bright side. You're in the small ghetto, intellectuals, professional people, you're better off than us. Here, in the large ghetto, it's a cesspool. But you, you're living in Monte Carlo. You could say you're privileged and that, of course, goes against my principles. Nevertheless –

He laughs and coughs, starts looking through papers. His room is piled from floor to ceiling with old papers and stuff. Dark, shabby, run-down.

One of his sons, Symche, is operating the mimeograph machine. The other, Dolek, is sorting the sheets as they come off the roller. Mrs Zyskind, holding a toddler, is cooking at a small stove.

Jehuda finds what he's been looking for, a newspaper made up of a few sheets.

JEHUDA

Ah, here. Today's news from the other side.

SZPILMAN

You're amazing, Yehuda.

JEHUDA

No, I'm a socialist. I have brothers everywhere. They bring me news and food. We care about our fellow human beings. Workers of the world unite.

SZPILMAN

So, what's the news?

JEHUDA
(*scanning the paper*)
The Germans are advancing on Kharkhov.

SZPILMAN

I don't know why I come here every evening, it's always such bad news –

JEHUDA

Bad news, you crazy? You have no world view, Wladek, that's your trouble. The news couldn't be better. The moment Hitler invaded Russia, I knew we'd be all right. Remember Napoleon. Same business. The Germans will freeze to death, please God.

He beams. Szpilman leans over, takes a sheet from the mimeograph.

SZPILMAN

Jehuda, give me something to do.

JEHUDA

You're an artist, Wladek, you keep people's spirits up. You do enough.

SZPILMAN

But I want to help, I want to –

JEHUDA

You're too well known, Wladek. And you know what? You musicians don't make good conspirators. You're too – too musical –

He loves this, laughs, coughs.

32

SZPILMAN

There are notices going up. The city's to be cleansed of undesirables.

JEHUDA

There are always notices going up.

A distinctive knock on the door. Szpilman tenses but Jehuda beams. To one of his boys:

Symche –

The boy opens the door to admit a short, neat man, Majorek.

MAJOREK

Hello, Symche, Dolek, Mrs Zyskind, Jehuda. Working hard?

He stops, seeing Szpilman.

JEHUDA

Majorek, this is the greatest pianist in Poland, maybe in the whole world. Wladyslaw Szpilman. Meet Majorek.

MAJOREK
(shakes Szpilman's hand)
I know your name. I've never heard you play –

JEHUDA

Majorek used to be in the army. Brilliant man. He's got a mind like a searchlight. The only thing I've got against him is he's not a socialist. (*He looks out of the window.*) You'd better go now, Wladek. It's nearly curfew. (*He hands over pamphlets to Majorek.*) You see these, Wladek? You know how many copies we print of our newspaper?

Szpilman shrugs.

Five hundred. You know how many people on average read one copy? Twenty. That makes ten thousand readers. These will start the uprising. Majorek hides them in his underpants. And leaves them in toilets.

SZPILMAN

Toilets?

MAJOREK

As many toilets as I can find. Germans never go into Jewish toilets. They're too clean for them.

Jehuda loves this too, but his laugh makes him cough appallingly.

INT. GHETTO APARTMENT — EVENING

Summer. The windows are open and the sounds of the ghetto can be heard in the background.

The family sit round the small table as Mother comes with a saucepan of soup and starts to serve.

MOTHER

And, please, tonight, for once, I don't want anything bad talked about. Let's enjoy our meal.

HENRYK

Okay, then I'll tell you something funny. You know who I mean by Dr Raszeja –

REGINA

The surgeon –

HENRYK

The surgeon. Well, for some reason, don't ask me why, the Germans allowed him into the ghetto to perform an operation –

HALINA

On a Jew? They allowed a Pole to come in to operate on a Jew?

HENRYK

He got a pass, that's all I know. Anyway, he puts the patient to sleep and starts the operation. He'd just made the first incision when the SS burst in, shoot the patient lying on the table, and then shoot Dr Raszeja and everybody else who was there. Isn't that a laugh? The patient didn't feel a thing, he was anaesthetised –

He laughs. No one else does.

MOTHER

Henryk, I said nothing bad –

HENRYK

What's the matter with you all? Have you lost your sense of humour –?

SZPILMAN

It's not funny –

HENRYK

Well, you know what's funny? You're funny with that ridiculous tie.

SZPILMAN

What are you talking about, my tie? What's my tie got to do with anything? I need the tie for my work –

MOTHER

Boys, boys –

HENRYK

Your work, yes, playing the piano for all the parasites in the ghetto, they don't give a damn about people's sufferings, they don't even notice what's going on around them –

FATHER

I blame the Americans.

The others look at him.

SZPILMAN

For what? For my tie?

FATHER

American Jews, and there's lots of them, what have they done for us? What do they think they're doing? People here are dying, haven't got a bite to eat. The Jewish bankers over there should be persuading America to declare war on Germany –

Suddenly, there's a roar of engines and a screech of brakes. Slamming of doors.

The family rush to the windows.

35

EXT./INT. BUILDING OPPOSITE AND GHETTO APARTMENT — NIGHT

A Gestapo vehicle has entered the street and screeched to a halt. Helmeted, jackbooted SS men, led by an NCO, pour out of the vehicle.

The Szpilmans gather at their open window to watch. Regina turns off the lights before joining them. They are all terrified. Their half-eaten meal still on the table behind them.

Point of view from Szpilman apartment: the building opposite.

The SS men pouring into the building opposite. Sound of the jackboots on stairs. Lights go on floor by floor.

In an apartment directly opposite, a businessman, his wife, three young people and an old man in a wheelchair sit at their dining table. The SS men burst in, machine pistols at the ready. The family is frozen with horror, remain seated.

The NCO scans their faces.

NCO
(in a towering rage)

Stand up!

The family rise to their feet fast, except for the old man in the wheelchair. The NCO bears down on him.

NCO

Stand up!

The old man in the wheelchair grips the arms of the chair and tries desperately to stand. But he can't. Without warning, the SS men seize the chair with the old man in it, carry him out on to the balcony.

The Szpilmans:

Mother screams, Father shrinks back, Halina comforts him and Regina comforts Mother.

Szpilman's and Henryk's point of view — the apartment opposite:

The SS men throw the old man in his wheelchair over the balcony. He seems to hang in the air for a second then drops out of the chair and out of sight. But there's a terrible thud as his body hits the pavement and a clatter as the wheelchair follows him.

The Szpilmans:

Mother sobbing. The others, still horrified.

REGINA
(softly, to Mother)

Be quiet, Mama, for God's sake, be quiet –

Then sound of shots, slamming doors, screams, shouts.

Szpilman and Henryk hurry to another window so that they can see what's going on.

Their point of view from second window – building opposite and street:

SS Men herding a couple of dozen prisoners from the building opposite.

People watching from the windows but trying not to be seen.

The headlights of the SS vehicle are switched on and the SS Men are forcing their prisoners to stand in the beam.

A GERMAN VOICE

Run! Run!

The prisoners start to run.

The SS men open fire with a machine gun mounted on the vehicle. People in the building opposite begin to scream.

The prisoners are being shot down. They are lifted into the air by the bullets, turn somersaults, fall dead.

One man escapes by running back in the opposite direction, out of the beam of light and is lost to sight for a moment.

The escaping man, a silhouette, out of the light, runs with all his strength, putting distance between himself and the SS. He starts to scale a wall. He looks as though he's getting away.

But there's a floodlight on the SS vehicle. It flares into light, swivels and finds the man. A volley of shots.

The man drops from the wall, dead.

The SS men get into the vehicle and speed off, driving over the dead bodies.

The Szpilmans:

Szpilman and Henryk stare at the scene, silent, shocked.

The only sounds, the weeping of the people opposite and, nearer, Mother crying softly.

INT. CAFÉ NOWOCZESNA — DAY

Szpilman, as if in another world, playing the piano. The café is full of customers but the atmosphere is much more subdued than previously, the mood is sombre.

EXT. CAFÉ NOWOCZESNA — DAY

A doorman with a cudgel beats away the beggars from the door as Halina, distraught and out of breath, runs to the café entrance. The doorman lets her in.

INT. CAFÉ NOWACZESNA — DAY

Szpilman snaps out of his reverie, seeing, across the heads of the customers, Halina, in a state of great anxiety, beckoning urgently.

Szpilman quickly brings the piece to a close, stands, steps off the platform, threads his way through to Halina. She's shivering, almost unable to speak.

SZPILMAN

What's happened?

HALINA
(almost incoherent)

Oh my God, it's terrible, you've got to do something, oh my God —

SZPILMAN
(shaking her)

Calm down, what, what is it?

HALINA

They're hunting people on the streets. They've picked up
Henryk –

EXT. STREETS — DAY

Szpilman running. Streets crowded. Corpses. Szpilman, sweating,
dodges and sidesteps. Then, suddenly, a woman bars his way. She's the
Feather Woman, brightly rouged, with her thickly painted eyebrows, the
unsteady mauve ostrich feather rising from her straw hat.

THE FEATHER WOMAN

Excuse me, but have you seen my husband Izaak Szerman?

SZPILMAN

I'm afraid not –

He tries to dodge past but she grabs his arm.

THE FEATHER WOMAN

He's tall, he's handsome. He has a little grey beard. If you
see him, please do write, Izaak Szerman's his name, don't
forget –

Szpilman manages to free himself and runs on.

EXT. LABOUR BUREAU BUILDING — DAY

A mob of men in front of the building being herded this way and that
by Jewish policemen. More and more captive men are brought in by
the German Schutzpolizei (Shupos). The mob constantly swelling.

Szpilman reaches the back of the crowd.

SZPILMAN
(to an elderly man nearest him)

What's happening?

THE ELDERLY MAN

They've got my grandson in there. They pick 'em up, they
take 'em away. What do they do to them? I've stopped
believing in God –

Szpilman scans the mob.

The Jewish policemen using batons and whips to herd the men. No sign of Henryk.

Szpilman becomes alert. He's seen someone he recognises.

Heller, with his red hair and Hitler moustache, wielding a baton, driving men into the building.

With difficulty, Szpilman pushes his way through the mob and gets nearer to Heller.

> SZPILMAN
> (*yelling*)

Yitzchak!

Heller doesn't hear.

Yitzchak!

Heller glances round.

Here, please! Wladek Szpilman!

Heller shoves someone aside so that Szpilman can approach, but he continues to beat and manhandle people.

> SZPILMAN

Henryk's in there –

> HELLER

I haven't seen him.

> SZPILMAN

Believe me, they've picked him up –

> HELLER

Tough luck –

> SZPILMAN

Can you help?

> HELLER

Oh, you need me now, yes, now you need me –

SZPILMAN

Can you help us?

HELLER

It costs.

SZPILMAN

I've no money –

HELLER

Then there's nothing I can do. He should've joined us
when I gave him the chance –

SZPILMAN

Yitzchak, they told me you had influence –

HELLER

Who told you?

SZPILMAN

People I know. They said you're an important man –

*Heller just glares at Szpilman and then moves away. Szpilman stands,
jostled by the crowd, uncertain, forlorn.*

EXT. ALLEY AND LABOUR BUREAU, LATER — MID-AFTERNOON

*Szpilman, keeping to the shadows of the alleyway, watches the front of
the building. Comings and goings. German soldiers in evidence. The
mob is smaller now.*

*Szpilman waits and watches, and then a poor woman passes, carrying
a can wrapped in newspaper followed by a ragged old man, dragging
himself along. He's shivering with cold, his shoes with holes show his
purple feet.*

*The ragged old man suddenly lunges forward and tries to grab the can
from the poor woman. They struggle desperately.*

POOR WOMAN
(*screaming*)
A snatcher! Help me, a snatcher!

The can falls to the pavement and thick, steaming soup pours into the dirty street.

Szpilman watches, rooted to the spot. The ragged old man stares at the can, lets out a groan, more like a whimper, and throws himself full length in the slush, licking the soup up from the pavement. The poor woman starts to howl, kicking the old man and tearing at her hair in despair.

Then:

RUBINSTEIN'S VOICE

Boys, keep your peckers up! And girls, keep your legs crossed!

Rubinstein, a ragged, dishevelled little man, Chaplinesque, waving a stick, hopping and jumping, approaches the Germans outside the bureau.

RUBINSTEIN

Don't let 'em get you down –

He approaches a couple of Shupos.

Bandits! Crooks! Thieves!

He waves his stick at them. They laugh. One of them bows low.

IST SHUPO

Good day, Herr Rubinstein –

RUBINSTEIN

If that means good day, I'm your man, you gangsters, robbers, pirates!

2ND SHUPO
(*tapping his head*)

Mad!

RUBINSTEIN

Ich bin meshuge, you bandit!

Almost in tears with laughter, they give him a cigarette and he goes on his way.

Szpilman almost smiles, then looks again at the building. He waits.

EXT. ALLEY AND LABOUR BUREAU, LATER — DUSK

Sun just setting.

From the shelter of the alleyway, Szpilman continues to watch the entrance of the bureau. No mob any more, but people come and go — Jewish policemen, Shupos, a few Jews.

Almost continuous sounds of distant shots and screams.

Then, Heller appears at the entrance, looks this way and that and goes back inside the building.

Szpilman alert.

Again Heller appears in the entrance. He beckons someone inside. Henryk shuffles out. Heller shoves him into the street. Henryk stumbles, falls.

Szpilman runs to him, helps him to his feet.

> HENRYK
> (*immediately on the attack, furious*)
> You go to Heller, did I ask you to talk to him?

> SZPILMAN
> You're out, aren't you?

They start to walk.

> HENRYK
> Did you beg, did you grovel to that piece of shit, that cockroach?

> SZPILMAN
> I didn't grovel, I asked him to help –

> HENRYK
> What did you pay him?

> SZPILMAN
> Pay him? With what? With what could I pay him? Every zloty I earn we spend on food –

> HENRYK
> I can look after myself –

                    SZPILMAN

They were taking you away –

                    HENRYK

It's nothing to do with you. It's me they wanted, not you.
Why do you interfere in other people's business?

                    SZPILMAN

You're mad, that's your trouble, you're mad.

                    HENRYK

That's also my business.

They walk on.

EXT. CHLODNA STREET BRIDGE – DUSK

*A wooden bridge has been constructed, linking the small ghetto to the
large ghetto. Few people about, mostly beggars and children.*

*Szpilman and Henryk climb the stairs of the bridge, but as they reach
the bridge itself Henryk stumbles, sinks to his knees. Szpilman gets
hold of him, tries to help him stand.*

                    SZPILMAN

What's the matter? Are you sick?

                    HENRYK

Hungry –

EXT. CAFÉ NOWOCZESNA – NIGHT

Szpilman supports Henryk, helps him towards the back of the café.

INT. KITCHEN, CAFÉ NOWOCZESNA – NIGHT

*Henryk, finishing a bowl of soup and a piece of bread, sits at a
worktop with Szpilman and Benek. The kitchen is small and busy
with cooks, waiters, washers-up.*

                    SZPILMAN

What's that mean, no employment certificate?

HENRYK

You have to have an employment certificate to work for one
of the German firms in the ghetto, otherwise –

SZPILMAN

Otherwise what?

HENRYK

You'll be deported.

BENEK

So the rumours were true –

HENRYK

They're going to resettle us. Send us to labour camps. In
the east. And they're closing the small ghetto.

Silence.

EXT. CHLODNA STREET – DAY

A dense crowd of people crossing the bridge in both directions.

*Szpilman, shabby and unshaven, hurries along and meets Jehuda
Zyskind coming towards him, accompanied by the small man,
Majorek.*

JEHUDA

Wladek!

Szpilman stops.

I thought you'd be off on tour, playing London, Paris, New
York –

SZPILMAN
(*trying to smile*)

Not this week.

*They're buffeted by the crowd. In the street below them, cars, trams,
pedestrians and German guards.*

JEHUDA

I have to say you look terrible. What's the trouble?

SZPILMAN

You've heard the rumours they're going to resettle us in the East?

JEHUDA
(*dismissing him*)
Rumours, rumours, you take it all too much to heart, Wladek –

SZPILMAN

I've been trying to get a certificate of employment for my father. I've managed to get certificates for me and the rest of the family but I need one more for my father. I've been trying all the firms, the shops –

JEHUDA

Why didn't you come to me?

SZPILMAN

I didn't know you were in the certificate business –

JEHUDA

I'm not, but Majorek is.

SZPILMAN
(*to Majorek*)
Can you help? I've no money –

JEHUDA

Please, don't insult us – (*to Majorek*) Can you do something for him?

MAJOREK

Be at the Schultz Workshop, tomorrow, four o'clock.

JEHUDA

You see what a wonderful piece of luck you've had today? That's the historical imperative in action and that's why I always say, look on –

SZPILMAN
(*joining with him*)
– the bright side, yes, I know.

INT. OFFICE AND FLOOR, SCHULTZ FACTORY — DAY

The name 'Samuel Szpilman' being written on a certificate. The clatter of sewing machines.

Schultz, a fat, sweaty German is filling out the form at his desk. Majorek beside him, standing, chatting to him and having a quiet laugh. In the doorway, Szpilman and Father.

The small office is on an upper level with a window looking down on the factory floor where Jewish men and women are hard at work on sewing machines making the terrible clatter.

Schultz stamps the certificate, hands it to Majorek, who gives it to Father.

> FATHER
> (*doffing his hat*)

Thank you.

> SCHULTZ
> (*beaming, German accent*)

My pleasure. It won't help you anyway –

EXT. CHLODNA STREET BRIDGE — DAY

A great mass of agitated people crossing only one way: from the small ghetto to the large ghetto, carrying their belongings. A German film crew records the scene.

The Szpilmans among the crowd, lugging suitcases and bundles, Henryk with a few books, Father carrying his violin case. They struggle across the bridge.

EXT./INT. YARD AND WAREHOUSE — DAY

A truck backing up. The tail-gate is opened to reveal a huge load of furniture, linen, clothing, mirrors, carpets, bedclothes. Three Jews inside the van start to unload the stuff, dumping it in the yard.

Other Jews stand ready to start sorting the load, among them the Szpilman family. Shupos and Jewish policemen supervise.

Each has their allotted task: Szpilman and Henryk sort out carpets,
Father mirrors, Regina linen, Halina and Mother, clothing.

The sounds of trains not far off.

They carry the stuff into the warehouse.

INT. WAREHOUSE — DAY

Szpilman and the others bring their piles of things into the warehouse,
which is crammed with similar objects, an Aladdin's cave.

The activity continuous.

INT. SLEEPING QUARTERS, ABOVE WAREHOUSE — NIGHT

Semi-darkness. A large room with an improvised partition of blankets
to separate the men from the women. Three-tiered bunks.

On the men's side, Father is on the upper bunk, Henryk on the lower.
Szpilman, stripping down to his underwear, is preparing to climb into
the middle bunk.

> FATHER
> At least we've got work in the ghetto. At least we're still
> together.

Szpilman nods, climbs into his bunk, settles down. Somewhere near,
the sound of a train.

Then a volley of shots, German voices shouting.

Szpilman slips off his bunk, hurries to the door, opens it and comes
face to face with a German NCO and soldiers.

> NCO
> Out! Assemble in the yard!

> SZPILMAN
> We're employed here, we've got certificates –

The NCO cracks Szpilman across the face, turns and goes.

Szpilman retreats into the room, his nose bleeding. The women are
watching from behind the blankets, but Mother hurries towards
Szpilman. She wipes his nose.

Shots, shouts, a scream.

EXT. WAREHOUSE YARD — DAWN

*Still quite dark. The Szpilmans and about twenty others lined up
under lights shining on them from a couple of German vehicles.*

*The NCO goes along the line, making a selection, using his pistol to
prod people into moving. When he gets to the Szpilmans he selects
Henryk and Halina. Then, he turns to those who are left:*

> NCO
> The rest of you get dressed then report back here. Bring
> your belongings. Fifteen kilos only.

> A YOUNG WOMAN
> Where are you taking us?

*The NCO turns his pistol on the young woman and shoots her
through the head. He marches off while she lies on the ground with
blood spurting out of her.*

INT. SZPILMAN ROOMS, WAREHOUSE — DAWN

*The partition has been pulled aside. People, including the Szpilmans,
are dressing or dressed, packing up their belongings.*

> SZPILMAN
> I'm sorry, I did my best, I thought the certificates would
> save us all —

> MOTHER
> Stop it, Wladek —

> REGINA
> Let's just hope that Henryk and Halina will be better off —

Sounds of shots, screams, shouts, a piercing whistle.

EXT. STREET LEADING TO UMSCHLAGPLATZ — MORNING

*Hot, fine summer's day. Jews, among them Szpilman, Mother, Regina
and Father, clutching their meagre belongings, walk towards wooden*

*gates and come to a halt. Jewish policemen approach and order the
people about, pushing and shoving them into line.*

REGINA
(*to a Jewish policeman*)
Where will we be going?

I JEWISH POLICEMAN
You're going to work. You'll be much better off than in this
stinking ghetto.

The gates are opened.

2 JEWISH POLICEMAN
Move!

They shuffle forward.

EXT. UMSCHLAGPLATZ – DAY

*Szpilman, Mother, Regina and Father, with others, enter through one
of the gates, which closes on them. They pause for a moment to take in
their new surroundings.*

The Szpilmans and their point of view:

*Their first sight of the large rectangle, walled on two sides and overlooked
by buildings. Several hundred people. People walk up and down.*

SZPILMAN
Let's sit over there –

*But he stops again, and so do the others. Something they see causes
them to stand stock still, expressionless.*

The Szpilmans' point of view:

*An unoccupied space at the edge of the compound where bloated,
decaying bodies lie near to a wall. The wall itself is spattered with
blood. Large flies walk over the dead. Nobody goes near. –*

The Szpilmans:

Szpilman turns away and leads the others to another space.

Later:

Glaring sun.

The Szpilmans have settled down on the kerb of a pavement and are waiting. Szpilman stands, observing the scene.

Mother sits on a bundle of things, staring vacantly, her hair hanging down in strands. Regina, beside her, has her hands over her face and is weeping, the tears running through her fingers.

Father walks nervously up and down, hands behind his back, four steps one way, four steps back.

Near them, a young woman begins to wail.

> THE YOUNG WOMAN
> Why did I do it? Why did I do it?

A young man, beside her, whispers to her, but she does not seem to take in what he's saying. Her cries continue at intervals.

> THE YOUNG WOMAN
> Why did I do it? Why did I do it?

The sound of trucks. Everyone looks towards the gates.

More Jews are being unloaded from trucks and are marched through the gates. Mothers, children, old people, begging, most of them holding papers. Pandemonium.

Later:

The sun high, blazing.

Szpilman is wandering around, occasionally greeting people. The place is crowded now, packed. Trucks bring more and more Jews at intervals.

Old people lying down, exhausted, impossible to tell whether some of them are alive or dead.

Women carrying dehydrated children drag themselves from group to group. One woman approaches Szpilman.

> WOMAN WITH CHILD
> He's dying, don't you have a drop of water? My child's dying of thirst, he's dying, he's dying, I beg you –

Szpilman shakes his head sadly. The woman with child wanders off to another group.

A MAN'S VOICE

I'm telling you, it's a disgrace.

Szpilman turns to see a man, Dr Ehrlich, haranguing Father.

FATHER

I can hear you –

Szpilman goes to them.

DR EHRLICH
(*overlapping*)

We're letting them take us to our death like sheep to the slaughter!

FATHER

Dr Ehrlich, not so loud –

DR EHRLICH

Why don't we attack them? There's half a million of us, we could break out of the ghetto. At least we could die honourably, not as a stain on the face of history!

Another man, Grün, joins in.

GRÜN

Why you so sure they're sending us to our death?

DR EHRLICH

I'm not sure. You know why I'm not sure? Because they didn't tell me. But I'm telling you they plan to wipe us all out!

FATHER

Dr Ehrlich, what do you want me to do? You want me to fight?

GRÜN

To fight you need organisation, plans, guns –

FATHER

He's right. What d'you think I can do? Fight them with my violin bow?

GRÜN

The Germans would never squander a huge labour force like this. They're sending us to a labour camp.

DR EHRLICH

Oh, sure. Look at that cripple, look at those old people, the children, they're going to work? Look at Mr Szpilman here, he's going to carry iron girders on his back?

A loud cry from Mother. Szpilman and Father spin round.

MOTHER

Henryk!

REGINA
(glancing up, shocked)
Oh my God –

Near the gates, among a large bunch of new arrivals, Henryk and Halina.

MOTHER

Halina! Henryk!

Regina and Szpilman also call and wave. Henryk and Halina struggle through to them. Halina falls into Mother's arms and they hug.

HALINA

We heard you were here – we – didn't want – we – we wanted to be with you –

Mother comforts her. And so does Regina. Father smiles sadly.

SZPILMAN
(shakes his head, almost to himself, a forlorn smile)
Stupid, stupid –

THE YOUNG WOMAN

Why did I do it? Why did I do it?

Szpilman stands and stares at her.

Later:

The sun lower but the heat still intense.

The place is now packed to suffocation. People calling out names, trying to find each other. The wailing of women and the cries of children.

A cordon of Jewish policemen and SS guards are, almost surreptitiously, ringing the compound.

The Szpilmans sit in the same place, with Henryk sitting a little apart and now reading a small book.

> THE YOUNG WOMAN
> Why did I do it? Why did I do it?

> HALINA
> She's getting on my nerves. What did she do, for God's sake?

Grün leans across to her.

> GRÜN
> *(quietly, to Halina)*
> She smothered her baby.

Halina looks at him in disbelief.

> They'd prepared a hiding place and so, of course, they went there. But the baby cried just as the police came. She smothered the cries with her hands. The baby died. A policeman heard the death rattle. He found where they were hiding.

Later:

Szpilman and Henryk.

> SZPILMAN
> What are you reading?

> HENRYK
> *(a crooked, ironic smile)*
> 'If you prick us, do we not bleed? If you tickle us, do we not laugh? If you poison us, do we not die? And if you wrong us, shall we not revenge?'

Szpilman takes the book and reads the title page: THE MERCHANT OF VENICE BY WILLIAM SHAKESPEARE.

SZPILMAN

Very appropriate.

HENRYK

(*taking the book back and resuming his reading*)

Yes, that's why I brought it.

Later:

The Szpilmans seated on the kerb. Their attention is caught by a boy who has a box of sweets on a string round his neck. And he's selling the sweets, pocketing money.

HENRYK

Idiot. What's he think he's going to do with the money?

Father calls to the Sweet Boy and beckons him over.

FATHER

How much for a caramel?

THE SWEET BOY

Twenty zlotys.

FATHER

What? For one caramel? What d'you think you're going to do with the money?

THE SWEET BOY

Twenty zlotys.

FATHER

(*turning to the family*)

Have we got twenty between us?

They search their pockets and handbags, hand over to Father what change they can find. He, in turn, hands the money to the Sweet Boy, who hands over one caramel and goes on his way.

Father holds the caramel between thumb and forefinger and examines it carefully. Then, carefully takes out his penknife and with great care divides the caramel into six parts. He hands a part to each of the family.

They all exchange a look, an acknowledgement of each other, almost like a toast, and then they chew, slowly, deliberately.

The whistle of a locomotive. Sound of trucks rattling over the rails.

At once, a sound of great agitation from the Jews in the compound.

EXT. RAILWAY SIDING — DAY

The locomotive pulling cattle and goods trucks comes into sight, rolling slowly towards the boundary of the Umschlagplatz and coming to a halt.

EXT. RAILWAY SIDING — DAY

A cordon of Jewish policeman and SS guards. Among the great throng of people, the Szpilmans trudge towards the train.

Szpilman and Halina walking.

> SZPILMAN
>
> Halina –?

> HALINA
>
> What?

> SZPILMAN
>
> Funny time to say this –

> HALINA
>
> What?

> SZPILMAN
>
> I wish I knew you better –

> HALINA
> (*a smile*)
>
> Thanks.

The train:

The Szpilmans near the train. The first trucks are already full, the people inside pressed close together, SS men pushing them with their rifle butts.

People in the trucks cry out in desperation.

The Szpilmans are pushed along by SS men along the cordon of Jewish policemen, past loaded trucks.

Then, suddenly:

A VOICE
Szpilman! Szpilman!

A Jewish policeman grabs Szpilman by his collar and pulls him back out of the police cordon. It's Heller. The rest of the family have reached the next truck to be filled.

A scuffle as Szpilman tries to resist. Another Jewish policeman shoves him.

Szpilman stumbles, falls to the ground, in front of him the closed ranks of the Jewish policemen's backs.

He stands, runs at the cordon, seeing between their heads, shoulders, Mother, Regina, Henryk and Halina clambering into the trucks. Father is looking around, bewildered.

SZPILMAN
(*yelling*)
Papa!

Father sees him, takes a step towards him, but stops, smiling helplessly. He raises his hand and waves, then turns and goes towards the trucks.

Again, Szpilman flings himself at the policemen's shoulders.

SZPILMAN
(*desperate*)
Papa! Mama! Halina!

Heller turns on him.

HELLER
What do you think you're doing, Szpilman? I've saved your life! Now, go on, save yourself!

Szpilman stands for a moment, confused, terrified. Then he turns and starts to run.

57

HELLER

Don't run!

Szpilman drops to walking pace, makes for the gates. Workers are pushing carts piled with the bloated corpses that lay against the wall. Szpilman falls in with them and they pass through the gates.

EXT. TRAIN — DAY

The doors of the trucks are closed. The train begins to move. Slow, laborious. From the trucks, the faint cries of the occupants.

EXT. STREET BY THE SIDING — DAY

Szpilman catches his breath by a building. An SS man and Jewish policeman emerge. The Jewish policeman is servile, crawling to the German. He points to the train —

JEWISH POLICEMAN

Well, off they go for meltdown!

They laugh as they walk away.

Szpilman turns and stumbles down the empty street. The cries from the trucks fading. He begins to weep, loud, agonised sobs, and staggers on.

EXT. GHETTO STREET — EVENING

Szpilman, lost, empty, aimless, tries to catch his breath in the aftermath of his tears.

He wanders forlornly down the street, passing empty buildings with their doors open, windows smashed. Furniture, torn mattresses and pillows lie scattered. Feathers fly. Desolation.

He turns a corner.

EXT. COURTYARD, JEHUDA'S STREET — EVENING

Szpilman comes into the courtyard. He stops, his face blank.

Lying outside the door, the bodies of Jehuda, Mrs Zyskind, their two sons and the toddler.

Szpilman steps across the bodies.

INT. JEHUDA ZYSKIND'S ROOM — EVENING

Chaos. Papers, pamphlets strewn all over the place. The mimeograph smashed.

Szpilman enters, stands, surveying the devastation.

Distant sounds of shooting, shouts, cries.

He gathers up some papers in a pile, takes off his jacket and covers the pile of papers, making a pillow. He lies down on the floor.

He stares into the darkness, expressionless, empty.

EXT. STREET NEAR CAFÉ NOWOCZESNA — DAY

Szpilman shuffles along, comes to the café. No sign of life, but the door is wide open. He goes inside.

INT. CAFÉ NOWOCZESNA — DAY

A shambles. Szpilman wanders through the upturned tables, broken chairs. Stops, looks about. Nothing.

Distant shots, automatic fire.

He turns and makes for the door.

Then he hears an urgent hiss. He turns sharply and tries to find the source of it. He hears the hiss again.

Now he sees, hiding under the platform, Benek, beckoning to him. Szpilman hurries over and crawls on his back until he's beside him. Benek replaces a plank and they are hidden from view.

INT. UNDER THE PLATFORM, GHETTO CAFÉ — DAY

Thin slivers of light illuminate the two men on their backs in the cramped space.

BENEK
(*looking at him, mystified*)
Why are you here, Mr Wladek?

SZPILMAN
It's like this – I – we – all of them –

He can't continue. Benek nods.

BENEK
Perhaps they're lucky. The quicker the better.

Brief pause.

It isn't over yet. We'll stay here for a couple of days. Until things die down.

Another pause.

I've bribed a policeman. He'll come when it's over.

EXT. GHETTO STREET – DAY

In bright sun, Szpilman and Benek march in a column, four abreast, under the command of two Jewish foremen, guarded by two German policemen. They are being marched out of the ghetto gates.

SZPILMAN
(*to Benek*)
My God. I haven't been outside for – it must be two years.

FELLOW WORKER
(*on the other side of him*)
Don't get over-excited.

EXT. ZELAZNA BRAMA SQUARE – DAY

Street traders with baskets full of wares, fruit, vegetables, fish, tins of preserves. Women bargain with them, making purchases. Lively, colourful. Dealers in gold and currency calling monotonously.

DEALERS
Gold, buy gold! Dollars! Roubles!

Later:

Szpilman, on top of a free-standing scaffold, Benek and the others demolishing a ghetto wall, wielding sledgehammers. They work slowly.

A smartly dressed young couple are passing, but stop.

They stare. The young woman is extremely attractive and knows it. The foremen, workers and the German policemen ogle her.

THE YOUNG WOMAN

Look – oh, do look!

Her young man is puzzled; she points.

Jews!

THE YOUNG MAN

Can't be the first time you've ever seen Jews –

Embarrassed, she giggles and they go. Szpilman, Benek and the others continue to work.

The foremen sit, sunning themselves, and the German policemen stand, deep in conversation, ignoring the workers.

Szpilman suddenly stops work. He has seen something in the square that alerts him.

At the furthest stall, he sees a woman, attractive, chic, in her thirties, buying vegetables at a stall. Het name is Janina Godlewska.

Surreptitiously, Szpilman raises a hand, trying to catch her attention. But he's frightened of alerting the German policemen and the foremen. Benek has noticed.

BENEK

Someone you know?

SZPILMAN

Yes.

Again Szpilman tries, but Janina, her profile to him, doesn't see.

BENEK

A beauty. Who is she?

SZPILMAN

A singer. Her husband's an actor. I knew them well. Good
people. I'd like to talk to her.

BENEK
(*playful*)
Don't forget, Mr Wladek, they hang them for helping Jews.

He goes back to work.

*The German policemen wander over to one of the stalls to buy fruit.
The moment they do so two Jewish workers scamper across to another
stall to buy bread.*

Szpilman glances across the square: Janina is still at the stall.

*He comes to a decision. He jumps down, is about to dash towards
Janina, but stops dead.*

Janina is no longer there.

EXT. GHETTO STREET — DAY

*As before, Szpilman and Benek march towards the ghetto gates in the
demolition column, four abreast, under the command of the Jewish
foremen and guarded by the two German policemen.*

Suddenly:

YOUNG SS MAN
Halt!

*The column halts before a young SS man, wild-eyed, with his sleeves
rolled up and wielding a pistol. He talks excitedly to the policemen
then turns, walks along the column dividing them up: some men to the
right, others, seven of them, to the left. Benek he orders to the left,
Szpilman to the right.*

Young SS man turns to those on the left.

Lie down!

*Terrified, they obey. He stands over them and, one by one, shoots them.
When he comes to Benek, the seventh man, his pistol runs out of
ammunition. He changes the clip, shoots Benek and marches off.*

EXT. BUILDING SITE, OUTSIDE GHETTO — DAY

Szpilman, bent almost double, carries a hod on his back piled with bricks. He is mounting a wooden ramp that runs up beside scaffolding on a small building site where an extra floor is being added to a house. There are Polish workers, too, who don't, of course, wear armbands as the Jews do. There's a wooden hut serving as a store on the site.

Halfway up the ramp, Szpilman hears someone whistle. He stops, turns to see, at the bottom of the ramp, Majorek, smiling and giving a discreet wave.

Later:

Szpilman and Majorek sip gruel out of mugs. They sit apart from the others who are also taking a break.

> SZPILMAN
>
> How long have you been here?

> MAJOREK
>
> Since last night. I was pleased to see you.

Brief silence.

> They're going to start the final resettlement now. We know what it means. We sent someone out. Zygmunt. A good man. His orders were to follow the trains out of Warsaw. He got to Sokolow. A local railwayman told him the tracks are divided, one branch leading to Treblinka. He said every day freight trains carrying people from Warsaw forked to Treblinka and returned empty. No transports of food are ever seen on that line. And civilians are forbidden to approach the Treblinka station. They're exterminating us. Won't take them long. We're sixty thousand left. Out of half a million. Mostly young people. And this time we're going to fight. We're in good shape. We're organised. We're prepared.

> SZPILMAN
>
> If you need help –

A whistle blows.

A little later:

Szpilman again mounting the ramp with a hod full of bricks on his back. The noise of airplanes overhead.

EXT. SKY — DAY

A swarm of Russian bombers. Anti-aircraft fire. Puffs of exploding shells.

EXT. BUILDING SITE — DAY

The workers look up. So does Szpilman and, as he does so, the bricks slide off his hod, crashing to the ground below.

>   ZICK-ZACK
> You!

An SS man, Zick-Zack (his nickname), with a whip, approaches Szpilman

> Here!

Szpilman goes to him. Enraged, Zick-Zack grabs him by the hair and presses his head hard between his thighs and then beats him mercilessly.

>   ZICK-ZACK
>   (with every stroke, hissing through clenched teeth)
> Und-zick! Und-zack! Und-zick! Und-zack!

After a dozen or so strokes, Szpilman falls forward and lies in the dirt. Zick-Zack nods, satisfied.

>   ZICK-ZACK
> Get him away from here.

Two Poles, without armbands, one of them Bartczak, drag him away.

Bartczak and the other man help Szpilman to his feet.

>   BARTCZAK
> Hope you played the piano better than you carry bricks.

POLISH WORKMAN
He won't last long if he goes on like this –

BARTCZAK
I'll see if I can get him something better –

INT./EXT. STORES AND BUILDING SITE – DAY

Winter. Rain. Cold. The store, a wooden hut, contains wood, nails, tools, paint, metal brackets.

Szpilman sits at a table, where a line of workers has formed. Szpilman makes a record in a ledger of the tools each worker takes out on the site.

A worker puts his head into the store.

WORKER
(*hissing*)
Trouble –

A GERMAN VOICE
Assemble! Fall in! Only the Jews! Poles go on working!
Only the Jews! Poles go on working!

The Jewish workers start to assemble on the site in haphazard ranks as an SS Captain strides in.

The SS Captain, with much jollity and jokes, hops up on to scaffolding and stands, beaming broadly, surveying the workers.

SS CAPTAIN
(*in English*)
I have important and good news for you. There are
rumours circulating that resettlement measures are again
going to be taken.

A glance between Szpilman and Majorek.

I want to assure you personally that no such measures will
be taken now or in the future. Posters will be going up also
to this effect. As proof of our good will, we want you to
select a delegate, who will be permitted to go into town
once a day to buy, on each worker's behalf, five kilos of

potatoes and one loaf of bread, which you will be allowed to take back into the ghetto. Now, why would we do that if we meant to resettle you?

He beams; no reaction from the workers.

You can do good business on what you don't eat. Isn't that what you Jews are best at? Making 'geld'?

Rubs thumb and forefinger and leers; still no reaction; his smile vanishes.

Carry on.

EXT. BUILDING SITE — DAY

Snow. Majorek pulls a barrow by a rope attached to its shaft across the site. On the barrow, five sacks. The Jewish workers are pleased to see him.

Majorek pulls the barrow to where Szpilman waits.

MAJOREK
(*under his breath*)
The smaller one. At the bottom.

Szpilman nods and starts unloading the sacks as Majorek moves away.

INT. STORES — DAY

Szpilman has unpacked the sacks and laid them in the corner. He kneels before the smallest of the sacks and unties the string around its neck.

He puts his hand inside the sack and potatoes tumble out. He reaches to the bottom and is still as his hand finds something. Carefully, he removes a pistol, then another, both wrapped in oil cloths. He hides them under his jacket.

INT./EXT. STORES AND BUILDING SITE — NIGHT

Szpilman and a Jewish worker distribute the potatoes to the other Jewish workers lined up with empty containers of various kinds. There are scales on the table, and they weigh out five kilos of potatoes, pour them into the men's containers and drop in a loaf of bread.

EXT. STREET LEADING TO GHETTO — NIGHT

The Jewish workers, all carrying their parcels of potatoes and bread, march back towards the ghetto gates escorted by two Polish policemen. Szpilman walks beside them. Ahead of him, Majorek near the front of the column.

As the column nears the ghetto gates, Majorek tosses his package over the wall and when Szpilman reaches the same spot, he throws a similar package. The column marches on.

INT. JEWISH BARRACKS — NIGHT

A small room with several three-tiered bunk beds. The sound of men's heavy breathing and snoring.

Szpilman lies awake, staring at the ceiling. He reaches inside his jacket, finds a scrap of paper and a pencil, writes something.

He slips off his bunk and crosses to another set of bunks, crouches down at the bottom one, where Majorek sleeps.

> SZPILMAN
> (*whispered*)

Majorek –

Majorek is instantly awake.

> I have a favour to ask. I want to get out of here –

> MAJOREK
> It's easy to get out, it's how you survive on the other side that's hard.

> SZPILMAN
> I know. But last summer, I worked for a day in Zelazna Brama Square. I saw someone I knew. A singer. Her husband's an actor. They're old friends. (*He holds out the piece of paper.*) I've written their names down. And their address. If they're still there. Janina Godlewska and Andrzej

Bogucki. Good people. Majorek, you go into the town every day. Would you try and make contact? Ask them if they'd help me get out of here?

Majorek takes the paper but says nothing. He turns over and goes back to sleep. Szpilman returns to his bunk.

INT. STORES — DAY

Szpilman has unloaded the sacks of potatoes into the corner and is kneeling, about to untie the string on the smallest sack. A sound alerts him. He looks round.

An SS Lieutenant has entered the stores, sucking his finger, which is bleeding.

SS LIEUTENANT
Any fucking plaster?

Szpilman immediately hurries to a cupboard, finds a First Aid tin, removes a plaster and gives it to the SS Lieutenant.

SS LIEUTENANT'S VOICE
(*while he applies the plaster to his finger*)
What were you up to?

Nothing from Szpilman.

What the fuck are those?

He indicates the sacks with his chin.

SZPILMAN
(*in German*)
We're allowed to take food into the ghetto. Five kilos of potatoes and a –

The SS Lieutenant walks over to the sacks and kicks the smallest one.

SS LIEUTENANT
Open it.

SZPILMAN
It's only potatoes and bread –

68

SS LIEUTENANT

Fuck that, you're lying, I can smell it. Open it.

Szpilman tries to untie the string, but he's too terrified and can't manage it. The SS Lieutenant shoves him out of the way, then takes from his belt a dagger and cuts the string.

The SS Lieutenant reaches in and withdraws a handful of long yellow beans. He glowers at Szpilman, reaches in again, produces a handful of oatmeal.

SS LIEUTENANT

You're all the same. Give a Jew a little finger, he takes the whole hand.

He throws the oatmeal in Szpilman's face.

You lie to me again and I'll shoot you personally.

He kicks Szpilman viciously and marches away.

Szpilman catches his breath, then quickly reaches into the bottom of the sack and finds a pistol and ammunition. He hides them under his clothes.

EXT. STREET LEADING TO GHETTO — NIGHT

Freezing cold. The Jewish workers, with their bundles of potatoes and bread, march back towards the ghetto gates escorted by the two Polish policemen. In the column, Szpilman, near the policeman with the moustache, and a little behind them, Majorek. Distant sounds of gunfire.

Majorek falls in beside Szpilman.

MAJOREK

I tried your friends. They're not at that address any more. But.

SZPILMAN

You made contact?

MAJOREK

Be ready to leave in two days' time. Same place as last night –

Sudden, frantic cries from the head of the column, which comes to a stop.

Two SS men, blind drunk, drinking vodka from bottles, are lashing the column with whips. One of them is Zick-Zack.

SZPILMAN

Oh, shit –

As the SS men advance on Szpilman and Majorek's section, Majorek slips back to his place in the column. Szpilman hides his package inside his coat.

Zick-Zack lashes out at the workers blindly.

ZICK-ZACK

Und-zick! Und-zack!

He takes a swig of vodka and comes face to face with Szpilman.

ZICK-ZACK
(*shouting*)

I'll soon teach you discipline! Jew pigs!

He is staring directly at Szpilman with glassy eyes. Szpilman is terrified, trying as surreptitiously as possible to cover his hidden package with his hands. A moment of danger. Zick-Zack grabs Szpilman by the collar.

Know why we beat you?

No response; shaking him.

Know why we beat you?

SZPILMAN
(*tentatively, in German*)

No. Why?

ZICK-ZACK

To celebrate New Year's Eve!

He and his comrade find this hilarious; recovering from his laughter.

Now, march! Go on, march!

The column starts to march.

And sing! (*He belches.*) Sing something cheerful! (*Laughs.*)
And sing it good and loud!

A brief silence, then from the back, a solo voice starts to sing, 'Children of Warsaw will go to fight!'

Szpilman glances back, sees that it's Majorek singing. Szpilman smiles, Majorek nods. Szpilman joins in. Now, so do the others.

They march on, singing lustily.

> Hey, ranks unite
> And follow the White Eagle!
> Stand up and fight
> Our mortal enemy.
> Riflemen, hey!
> Let's give them fire and brimstone.
> We'll blow away
> The yoke of slavery.
> Punish and rout
> The rapists of our nation.
> We'll smash the knout
> To save our dignity.
> Soon we'll be proud
> Of our liberation –
>
> Hey, take your sights!
> Aim sharply at the heart.
> Hey, load! Hey, shoot!
> Hey, load! Hey, shoot!
> Give 'em a bloody start!
> Hey, load! Hey, shoot!
> Aim sharply at the heart.

The column reaches the lamp posts near the ghetto gates. Szpilman throws his package over the wall. So does Majorek.

INT./EXT. STORES AND BUILDING SITE – EVENING

The Jewish workers lined up to get their potatoes and bread. Szpilman and two others weigh the potatoes.

Get on with it and fall in! Fall in!

Calmly, Szpilman leaves the table with the scales, walks past Majorek and the others, who, having got their potatoes, are assembling in a column, preparing to march back into the ghetto. The Polish workers have packed up their tools and are talking among themselves, also about to leave the site but in a casual way.

The SS guards shout orders for the Jewish column to move off. Szpilman seems as if he's going to join them, but at the last moment turns and falls in with the Polish workers, beside Barczak, who just glances at him then moves so that Szpilman is in the middle of the group.

Szpilman slips off his armband, stuffs it into his pocket.

The group walk into the darkness.

EXT. WISNIOWA STREET — NIGHT

Dimly lit. Empty street. Szpilman walks fast to the corner, stops, looks round anxiously. Nothing. He takes the armband from his pocket and drops it through the grating of a drain in the gutter just as there's movement in a darkened doorway. Szpilman tenses.

Then, out of the darkness of the doorway, a woman: Janina Godlewska.

She turns and starts to walk quickly. Szpilman, putting the collar of his coat up, follows, keeping pace. A pedestrian walks past in the opposite direction but pays them no attention.

Janina and Szpilman walk on.

EXT. BOGUCKI BUILDING — NIGHT

Janina comes to the front door, opens it with a key, goes in. Szpilman, a little distance behind, catches up and follows her inside.

INT. HALL, STAIRS AND 3RD FLOOR, BOGUCKI BUILDING —
NIGHT

Janina waits as Szpilman closes the front door, then starts up the stairs. Szpilman follows. She stops, turns to him, smiles, kisses him on the cheek, then continues up the stairs.

INT. BOGUCKI APARTMENT — NIGHT

Andrzej Bogucki, a handsome man, fortyish, tries to conceal his sense of shock at seeing Szpilman He holds out his hand and Szpilman shakes it.

Szpilman looks around the nicely furnished, large apartment. He looks at Bogucki and Janina. Tears well up in his eyes. He fights it hard, not to cry. So does Janina.

> BOGUCKI
> We haven't much time –

INT. SMALL BATHROOM, BOGUCKI APARTMENT — NIGHT

Szpilman lies in a steaming bath, eyes closed, as though he's in a trance.

A gentle knock on the door and Bogucki slips in with some clothes. He gazes at Szpilman, whose eyes remain closed.

> BOGUCKI
> You must hurry.

Bogucki holds up a towel. Szpilman lifts himself out of the bath and dries himself.

> BOGUCKI
> We're going to have to keep moving you. The Germans are hunting down indiscriminately now. Jews, non-Jews, anybody, everybody. (*handing him the clothes*) See if these fit. And, Wladek, you'd better shave. Use my razor. In the cabinet –

INT. LIVING ROOM, BOGUCKI APARTMENT — LATER

The ceramic stove. Szpilman's ghetto clothes, torn into strips, are being stuffed into it and burned.

Janina shoves the strips of clothes into the stove. Szpilman, now wearing Bogucki's suit and clean-shaven, watches the clothes burn while he spoons hot soup into his mouth.

SZPILMAN

Thank you, I don't.

BOGUCKI

You'll be looked after by Mr Gebczynski. He's on the other side of town. You'll stay there tonight. Then we'll find you somewhere else.

Janina adds the last strip of clothing.

JANINA

I'll bring you food.

BOGUCKI

Let's go —

EXT. WARSAW STREETS — NIGHT

A rickshaw carrying Szpilman and Bogucki travels along the dark streets.

EXT. GEBCZYNSKI'S STORE — NIGHT

The rickshaw comes to a halt outside a store. The moment it stops the shutters of the store are raised and Bogucki escorts Szpilman to the door, then quickly returns to the rickshaw, which moves off fast.

INT. GEBCZYNSKI'S STORE — NIGHT

Gebcznyski shakes hands with Szpilman, ushers him in and then pulls down the shutter.

Gebcznyski's store is for sanitary furnishings and supplies: lavatories, basins, baths, taps etc.

GEBCZYNSKI

I'll show you where you're going to sleep –

He leads the way and as he goes he picks up a cushion from a chair and a blanket. Szpilman follows.

Stairs to basement:

Gebczynski leads Szpilman down the stairs.

Basement store room:

Dark, shadowy. Shelves with taps, washers, pipes. Gebczynski leads the way to a particular set of shelves. He puts aside the cushion and blanket, then starts to push at the shelves. Szpilman, although puzzled, helps. Slowly, the shelves move to reveal a secret compartment.

GEBCZYNSKI

It's not going to be very comfortable.

SZPILMAN

I'll be fine.

GEBCZYNSKI

You'll have to stay here until tomorrow afternoon.

He helps Szpilman into the compartment.

We've got a flat for you. Near the ghetto wall. But it's safe.

He hands over the cushion and the blanket to Szpilman; then, putting his back to the shelves and his feet against the wall, he pushes the shelves back into place so that Szpilman is now hidden.

INT. SECRET COMPARTMENT – NIGHT

In the cramped space, Szpilman is not quite able to stretch full out. With difficulty, he puts the cushion behind his head, starts to cover himself with the blanket but stops, seeing something.

In niches, neatly stacked: rifles, pistols, grenades, ammunition.

Szpilman stares, expressionless.

EXT. TRAM STOP, WARSAW STREET — AFTERNOON

Szpilman and Gebczynski wait with others at the stop as the tram trundles towards them and comes to a halt.

As they board:

> GEBCZYNSKI
> (*quietly, to Szpilman*)
> Go as near to the front as possible, to the German section –

INT. TRAM (TRAVELLING) — AFTERNOON

Gebczynski and Szpilman apprehensive, push through the rear section, packed with Poles, seated and standing, until they reach a chain and a sign:

GERMANS ONLY

In the German section, only three or four passengers. Some read newspapers, others stare into space or out of the windows, but never looking at the Poles.

Szpilman tries to appear as inconspicuous as possible. The tram rumbles on its way.

INT. 1ST APARTMENT, 4TH FLOOR LANDING AND DOOR — AFTERNOON

Gebczynski and Szpilman come up the stairs to the landing and to a door. Gebczynski unlocks the door and they go in.

INT./EXT. 1ST APARTMENT, 4TH FLOOR, AND GHETTO — AFTERNOON

A charmingly furnished bed-sitting room with a comfortable divan. Gebczynski leads the way in. Szpilman glances around, goes to the window, looks out.

Szpilman and his point of view:

He can see a section of ghetto wall below. Beyond it, inside the ghetto, a narrow street leading to deserted buildings. Gebczynski comes up behind him.

GEBCZYNSKI

Must feel better this side of the wall.

SZPILMAN

Yes, but sometimes I'm still not sure which side of the wall
I'm on.

GEBCZYNSKI

Here –

He leads Szpilman to the small kitchen.

Gebczynski opens a cupboard to reveal potatoes, bread.

GEBCZYNSKI

I'll come again. And Janina Bogucki will visit twice a week.
Bring more food. See how you are.

He closes the cupboard.

The main room.

Gebczynski makes for the front door, stops.

GEBCZYNSKI

Yes, now, this is very important. In case of emergency,
I mean emergency, go to this address –

*He hands over a scrap of paper, shakes Szpilman's hand and goes
quickly.*

*Alone, Szpilman stands, lost for a moment. Then, he takes off his shoe
and stuffs the scrap of paper into it. While he does so, his eyes light on
the divan bed.*

*He goes to it, slips off his other shoe and lies down, testing the divan's
springiness with his whole body.*

He smiles beatifically. He shuts his eyes and is instantly asleep.

INT./EXT. IST APARTMENT — DAY

*Szpilman still fast asleep. Voices wake him. He opens his eyes. He's not
certain where he is for a moment.*

He hears the voices again, coming from the adjoining flat.

77

Intrigued, he rises, goes closer to the wall, puts his ear against it, listens. After a brief silence:

> KITTEN'S VOICE
> *(angry)*
> Puppydog, what d'you mean, you forgot?

> PUPPYDOG'S VOICE
> What d'you think I mean, Kitten? I forgot, that's what I mean.

> KITTEN'S VOICE
> You know what? You treat me like dirt!

> PUPPYDOG'S VOICE
> I treat you like dirt because you are dirt.

> KITTEN'S VOICE
> Pig!

> PUPPYDOG'S VOICE
> Cow!

> KITTEN'S VOICE
> Pig!

> PUPPYDOG'S VOICE
> Bitch!

> KITTEN'S VOICE
> Dirty pig!

> PUPPYDOG'S VOICE
> You're a dirty pig!

> KITTEN'S VOICE
> Takes one to know one! Pig!

Silence. Szpilman is enjoying himself.

Then the sound of a piano being played with great feeling but a lot of wrong notes.

> PUPPYDOG'S VOICE
> You play like an angel, Kitten.

The piano continues for a moment, but suddenly stops:

>   KITTEN'S VOICE
> If I play like an angel, why don't you listen?

>   PUPPYDOG'S VOICE
> I was listening, Kitten –

>   KITTEN'S VOICE
> Liar, you fell asleep. Pig!

A door slams.

>   PUPPYDOG'S VOICE
>   (*wheedling*)
> Kitten, let me in.

Silence. Szpilman smiles but then hears the sound of rifle shots and a huge explosion.

He crosses quickly to the window, looks out.

Szpilman and his point of view – the ghetto.

Deserted. Stillness. Silence. From the ghetto smoke drifting slowly.

INT./EXT. IST APARTMENT — EARLY MORNING

Szpilman asleep on the divan. The roar of motor car and motorcycle engines. Sporadic firing.

He wakes, rushes to the window.

Szpilman and his point of view:

A German personnel carrier, an open car carrying officers, and a motorcycle and sidecar roar down the narrow street below towards the buildings at the far end. German soldiers follow behind on the trot, pulling a field gun.

Unseen marksmen fire down on the Germans from the buildings. As the German soldiers dismount from their vehicles one of them is hit and falls. The others rush for cover.

EXT. INSIDE THE GHETTO — MINUTES LATER — EARLY MORNING

The German Commander and two officers alight from the car and take cover.

The Commander orders the field gun to be trained on the buildings. Spasmodic firing continues.

He gives the order to fire.

The gun roars. The shell tears into the building. At once the German soldiers open fire with their rifles and lob grenades into the building. The gun fires again.

The building begins to burn. Flames and smoke.

German soldiers with flame-throwers advance carefully then unleash their fire into doorways and windows, and quickly retreat.

At ground level, Jewish fighters try to fight their way out and are mowed down.

The fire spreads quickly through the building. Smoke begins to pour from the upper floors.

The Germans, less cautious now, stand and watch.

A woman struggles out on to her narrow third-floor balcony. She climbs over, holds on to the wrought-iron railings and hangs on for dear life. Shots ring out and she drops like a stone.

From inside the building, screams and shouts.

From another upper window, a man in flames jumps and falls to his death on the pavement below.

The Germans have stopped firing. They stand, spectators, watching the building burn.

INT./EXT. IST APARTMENT — LATER — DAY

Szpilman at the window, watching, his mood downcast.

The noise of a key in the door.

He turns to see the door of the flat open. Janina enters with a parcel of food. She kisses Szpilman on the cheek.

JANINA

I wanted to come earlier but –

She hands him the parcel.

SZPILMAN

Thank you –

He goes into the small kitchen and unpacks the contents while Janina gazes out of the window.

JANINA

No one thought they'd hold out so long.

SZPILMAN

I should never have come out. I should've stayed there, fought with them –

JANINA
(*turning to him*)

Wladek, stop that. It's over now. Just be proud it happened. My God, did they put up a fight.

SZPILMAN

Yes, so did the Germans.

JANINA

They're in shock. They didn't expect it. Nobody expected it. Jews fighting back? Who'd have thought –?

SZPILMAN

Yes, but what good did it do?

JANINA
(*passionate*)

What good? Wladek, I'm surprised at you. They died with dignity, that's what good it did. And you know something else? Now the Poles will rise. We're ready. We'll fight, too. You'll see.

She turns to look again out of the window.

EXT. INSIDE THE GHETTO — EVENING

The building burning. Corpses lie scattered on the pavement. The Germans stand about chatting and laughing.

A handful of Jewish fighters are lined up and shot.

Satisfied, the Commander returns to his car. Another officer confers with him before the engine starts up and he is driven away. The building burns.

EXT. 1ST APARTMENT, SZPILMAN'S POINT OF VIEW — DAY

Blazing sun. The ghetto buildings now burned-out shells, the street empty.

EXT. 1ST APARTMENT — SZPILMAN AND HIS POINT OF VIEW — DAY

Autumn leaves falling and gusting in the wind. Szpilman gazes out.

EXT./INT. 1ST APARTMENT — DAY

Snow. Ice on the windows.

The sound of the key in the door.

Szpilman turns as the door opens and Gebczynski enters, distraught. Whispered, at speed:

> GEBCZYNSKI
> Get your things together, you have to leave –

> SZPILMAN
> What's happened?

Gebczynski takes out a cigarette and lights it. While he does so:

> GEBCZYNSKI
> I'm on the run –

> SZPILMAN
> What's happened?

GEBCZYNSKI

The Gestapo found our weapons. They've arrested Janina
and Andrzej. They're bound to find out about this place,
too – you must get away at once.

SZPILMAN

Where do you want me to go? Look at me. No, no, I'm not
leaving. Can't I take my chances here?

GEBCZYNSKI

That's your decision. (*Stubs out cigarette.*) But when they
storm the flat, throw yourself out of the window – don't let
them get you alive. I have poison on me, they won't get me
alive either –

*And he goes. Szpilman listens to his footsteps clattering down the
stairs.*

He sees the cigarette stub, takes it, lights it, coughs, smokes awkwardly.

Later:

*Szpilman hears a car engine and the screech of brakes. He tenses.
German voices shouting and their heavy footsteps on the stairs.*

*He goes to the window, opens it. He gets a chair, places it sideways
in front of the window to make a step. He's working out how best to
throw himself out.*

He leans against the wall near the door and waits..

Slamming of doors, German shouts, a scream.

Szpilman steels himself, ready to jump.

Again footsteps on the stairs, but this time descending. A door slams.

He cautiously goes to the window and looks out.

INT./EXT. 1ST APARTMENT – DAY

Szpilman and his point of view – the street.

*In the street below, he sees SS men escorting two prisoners and shoving
them into a car. The car speeds off. The street is empty.*

INT. 1ST APARTMENT — DUSK

Snow. Howling wind.

Szpilman lies on the divan. He is cold, unshaven, hair filthy and long. He manages to rise.

The small kitchen.

A mess. Szpilman goes into the kitchen. From a bread tin he takes a small, flat greaseproof paper parcel and unwraps it. A slice of bread, stale and mouldy. He tries to bite it but can't. He finds a knife and tries to chop a piece off the bread but knocks the bread tin, which falls to the floor with a clatter.

He continues to try to cut the bread, when there's a loud hammering on the front door.

Szpilman stiffens.

The living room.

The hammering continues as Szpilman stumbles into the room, looks around, confused, not knowing what to do.

From the other side of the door female voices, words indistinct, and then:

> KITTY'S VOICE
> Open this door at once, or we'll call the police!

He is galvanised into action, puts on a crumpled jacket, grabs his tattered coat and scarf, collects up a few of his things, stuffs them into a paper bag.

The hammering stops.

Szpilman cautiously approaches the door, listens, then opens it quietly and slips out.

INT. 1ST APARTMENT, LANDING AND DOOR — DUSK

He slips out of the flat, goes to the stairs and stops dead.

Kitty, young and fierce, stands on the stairs, blocking his way.

                              KITTY
Are you from the flat in there? You're not registered.

                            SZPILMAN
It belongs to a friend of mine. I came to visit but I must
have just missed him.

                              KITTY
                            (*shouting*)
Have you got your identity card? Let me see your identity
card!

Szpilman hesitates; she shouts more loudly.

I want to see your identity card!

*On various floors, doors open, tenants put their heads out to see what's
going on.*

*Summoning all his strength, Szpilman makes a dash for it, pushing
past Kitty.*

                              KITTY
                           (*screeching*)
He's a Jew! He's a Jew! Stop the Jew! Don't let him out!

*Szpilman clatters down the stairs, reaches the ground-floor landing.
Another woman tries to bar his way but he pushes past her and out
of the house.*

EXT. STREET — EVENING

*Heavy snow. Szpilman stumbles into the street and runs. He darts
down a side street.*

EXT. SIDE STREET — EVENING

*Szpilman lurches into the narrow street. No one about. He stops,
almost collapses, but manages to keep hold of himself. He puts on his
coat and wraps the scarf round his neck. He leans up against a wall.*

*He removes a shoe and takes out the scrap of paper Gebczynski gave
him. He reads it.*

EXT. NARBUTT STREET — NIGHT

Szpilman drags himself along, trudging through snow and slush.
Passers-by give him a wide berth. He tries to walk normally, with
dignity, but he's weak and slips, and finds the going hard.

He comes to a villa.

INT. VILLA, NARBUTT STREET — NIGHT

He goes to the front door, rings the bell and waits.

> WOMAN'S VOICE
> (*from behind the door*)

Yes?

> SZPILMAN

Mr Gebczynski sent me.

The door opens and Dorota stands there. She is pregnant.

They stand for a moment staring at each other.

> DOROTA
> (*a whisper*)

Wladyslaw Szpilman.

> SZPILMAN

Dorota.

> DOROTA

Come in – come in –

INT. DOROTA'S VILLA — NIGHT

Szpilman follows Dorota into the living room.

> DOROTA

Sit –

> SZPILMAN

I'm sorry – I was given this address. I'm looking for a Mr –
(*He checks the scrap of paper.*) – a Mr Dzikiewicz.

DOROTA
(nodding)

Michal Dzikiewicz. He's my husband.

Szpilman sits down slowly.

SZPILMAN

I need help.

DOROTA

He'll be back before curfew.

SZPILMAN

I've been in hiding. I need somewhere to stay.

DOROTA

He'll be here soon.

Awkward silence. He gazes at her. She looks away.

SZPILMAN

How long have you been married?

DOROTA

Just over a year.

He nods.

Brief silence.

SZPILMAN

And how's Yurek?

DOROTA

Dead.

Again, the awkward silence.

SZPILMAN

When's your baby due?

DOROTA

Christmas.

A pause.

This is not a good time to have children. But then –

87

The door opens and Michal Dzikiewicz enters. He sees Szpilman and stops. Szpilman stands.

DOROTA

This is my husband. Wladyslaw Szpilman– Marek Gebczynski sent him –

MICHAL

Oh, yes. I remember.

He shakes hands with Szpilman.

SZPILMAN

Mr Gebczynski said to contact you only in an emergency, but –

MICHAL

Don't worry now. We can't move you tonight.

Szpilman, dizzy, leans on the table for support.

You'll sleep on the sofa –

He and Dorota look at him.

SZPILMAN

Excuse me – could I have a piece of bread?

MICHAL

Yes, of course, we'll eat –

INT. DOROTA'S VILLA – MORNING

Szpilman asleep on the sofa. The sound of a cello. He opens his eyes. Listens.

He swings his legs off the sofa, stands, and crosses to a door. Quietly, he opens it a little.

Szpilman and his point of view – another room.

Dorota, partially turned away from him, plays Bach on the cello.

Szpilman watches her and listens.

INT. 2ND APARTMENT (4TH FLOOR), LANDING AND DOOR — NIGHT

A padlock being unlocked. Then, a key is inserted into the Yale lock, turned, and the door opens.

Michal and Szpilman on the landing, enter the flat.

INT./EXT. 2ND APARTMENT AND STREET — NIGHT

A large room, sparsely furnished but with an upright piano and a bed.

Michal carries a bag of provisions and puts them on a table while Szpilman goes immediately to the window and looks out.

Szpilman and his point of view:

There are views of the city, but in the street below, opposite, is a hospital and, on the corner, a building flying a Nazi flag and guarded by a sentry, standing at his sentry-box

Michal comes up behind Szpilman.

> MICHAL
> (*in whisper*)
> You're in a very German area. The building opposite is a hospital, taking in wounded from the Russian front. Next door is the Schutzpolizei. It's the safest place to be. Right in the centre of the lion's den.

The apartment:

Michal makes for the door.

> MICHAL
> I'll be locking you in. No one knows you're here. So keep as quiet as possible.

He nods and goes. The sound of the padlock closing.

Szpilman takes in the room. He sees the piano, is still for a moment, then goes to it.

He sits on the piano stool and adjusts its height. He opens the lid. A cloth covers the keys. He removes the cloth. He gazes lovingly at the keyboard. He flexes his fingers.

Then, without touching the keys, his fingers floating just above them, he plays. Silently. Passionately.

EXT. CITY SKYLINE. POINT OF VIEW THROUGH WINDOW — DAY

Snow falling.

INT. 2ND APARTMENT — DAY

Szpilman alert, hearing the padlock being unlocked and then the Yale. The door opens and Michal enters, accompanied by a man, aged about thirty, Szalas, confident, a little brash.

In whispers:

> MICHAL
>
> All well?

> SZPILMAN
>
> Thank you –

> MICHAL
>
> This is Antek Szalas.

Szalas and Szpilman shake hands.

> He's going to look after you. I've given him a second key. He'll bring you food. See that you're all right. He's with the underground, a good man –

Szalas produces a quarter bottle of vodka, thumps the back of the bottle so that the cork flies out. He finds glasses and pours. While he does all this:

> SZALAS
>
> You don't remember me, Mr Szpilman –

> SZPILMAN
>
> No, I don't think so –

> SZALAS
>
> Warsaw Radio. I was a technician. I saw you almost every day.

SZPILMAN

Sorry, I don't remember –

SZALAS

Doesn't matter. You've nothing to worry about. I'll visit often.

MICHAL

And you'll be pleased to hear the Allies are bombing Germany night after night – Cologne, Hamburg, Berlin.

SZALAS

And the Russians are really giving them hell. It's the beginning of the end.

He gives the others their vodka.

MICHAL

Let's hope so. I don't know when I'll see you again –

They clink glasses and drink.

EXT. 2ND APARTMENT – DAY

Summer. Trees in leaf.

Comings and goings at the Schutzpolizei building. And an ambulance draws up at the hospital, disgorging a couple of stretcher cases, who are carried inside.

INT. 2ND APARTMENT – DAY

Szilman, very weak and his skin yellowish, drops four beans into boiling water.

The sound of the padlock being opened.

Szpilman hurries to see the door open and Szalas enter with a small package and grinning cheerfully.

In whispers:

SZALAS

Still alive then, are you? Here. Sausage. Bread.

He hands over the package.

You still got that vodka?

Szpilman stares at the package.

SZPILMAN

How long is this meant to last?

Szalas shrugs, finds the vodka, pours two glasses.

SZPILMAN

I think I've got jaundice –

He unwraps the package to reveal sausage and bread. He takes a bite of sausage, chewing deliberately, slowly.

SZALAS

You don't want to worry about that. My grandfather was jilted by his girl friend when he got jaundice. (*Chuckles.*) In my opinion, jaundice is not very serious. Drink up.

SZPILMAN

Why didn't you come sooner? It's been over two weeks.

Szalas goes to the window, looks out.

SZALAS

Problems. Money. I've got to raise money to buy the food. I need things to sell, it' s not easy –

Szpilman thinks for a moment, then takes off his wristwatch, hands it to Szalas.

SZPILMAN

Sell this. Food's more important than time.

Szalas pockets the watch, makes for the door, stops –

SZALAS

Oh, yes. I meant to tell you. The Allies have landed in France. The Russians'll be here soon. They'll beat the shit out of the Germans. Any day now.

He grins, downs Szpilman's vodka, gives a mock salute and goes. The padlock is locked on the other side. Szpilman enjoys his sausage.

INT. 2ND APARTMENT — DAY

Sunshine floods in through the windows.

Szpilman lies inert on the bed, weak, starving, ill.

The sound of the padlock. He doesn't stir.

Dorota, no longer pregnant, and Michal enter, come to the bed.

In whispers:

> DOROTA
>
> Wladek? Wladek! (*to Michal*) I knew it, I knew this would
> happen –

*Szpilman barely has strength to open his eyes and focus on them. He
mutters incoherently.*

> I'm going to get a doctor –

> MICHAL
>
> You can't, it's too dangerous –

> DOROTA
>
> I'll get Dr Luczak, we can trust him –

> MICHAL
>
> Dorota, don't be ridiculous, he's a pediatrician –

> DOROTA
>
> He's still a doctor –

She starts for the door.

> MICHAL
>
> No, you stay, I'll go.

He leaves. The padlock sound.

*Dorota goes to the kitchen, wets a towel, comes back to the bed, kneels
beside it, places the towel on Szpilman's brow. He focuses on her,
smiles.*

> DOROTA
>
> We came to say goodbye. We're going to stay with my
> mother in Otwock. The baby's already there. It's safer.
> There's talk that the uprising will begin any day now.

Szpilman suddenly winces with pain.

> That man Szalas should be shot. He's been collecting money on your behalf all over Warsaw. Apparently, people gave generously. So he collected a tidy sum. He told us he was visiting you daily.

She looks at him; barely audible.

> Oh God –

Later:

Szpilman looks up at Dr Luczak, who has a stethoscope in his ears. Dorota and Michal stand behind him.

DOCTOR
Acute inflammation of the gall bladder. Liver the size of a football. But he'll live. I'll try to get hold of some levulose, but it's not easy.

DOROTA
Can you visit him again?

DOCTOR
Who knows?

SZPILMAN
Doctor, thank you –

DOCTOR
Don't speak. Rest.

The Doctor and Michal leave his line of vision.

Dorota moves in beside him.

DOROTA
Michal brought food. I'll prepare something now for you, then we must go.

Szpilman tries again to say something, but he can't, just lies there, distressed.

EXT./INT. APARTMENT — SZPILMAN AND HIS POINT OF VIEW — DAY

Szpilman looking down from the fourth-floor window. Peaceful. A few pedestrians. An everyday atmosphere.

At the far end, at the T-junction with a main road, a tram rumbles down the street and comes to a halt, disgorging passengers on the far side and so out of sight.

The tram continues on its way, now revealing the few passengers who alighted – women, an old man with a stick. Last, three young Poles, carrying long objects wrapped in newspaper.

One of the men looks at his watch, glances around, then suddenly kneels and puts the package he's carrying to his shoulder. The sound of rapid firing, which makes the newspaper at the end of the packet glow to reveal the barrel of a machine gun.

His two companions have also put their packages to their shoulders and begin shooting, all aiming their fire at the Schutzpolizei building.

The sentry is hit and falls in front of his box.

As if these young men have given a signal, now from all over the city comes the sound of gunfire.

The pedestrians have scattered except for the old man, gasping for breath, hobbling on his walking stick, who eventually manages to disappear inside a building.

Rifle and machine-gun fire from the Schutzpolizei building.

The firing intense. The three young Poles manoeuvre to the corner opposite the Schutzpolizei and toss grenades into the building.

EXT. DOWN IN THE STREET — DAY

A battle raging.

The Germans firing from the hospital.

The three young Poles have been joined by other fighters and they attack the Schutzpolizei building.

Grenades thrown, machine-gun fire exchanged.

The sentry box blows up, splinters of wood cascading.

A couple of Poles make a dash for it and enter a building opposite to the Schutzpolizei.

EXT./INT. 2ND APARTMENT — SZPILMAN AND HIS POINT OF
VIEW — DAY

Szpilman watching from his window, looks in the opposite direction and sees smoke rising.

When he turns back to look towards the T-junction, he sees a Panzerfaust anti-tank rocket firer poking out from a window in the next-door building but on the floor below.

The Panzerfaust fires. The shell hits the hospital.

EXT. CITY SKYLINE — NIGHT

The city in flames.

Sound of firing becoming sporadic, less intense. Isolated explosions.

INT. 2ND APARTMENT — NIGHT

Szpilman, lying on the bed, staring at the ceiling.

EXT. 2ND APARTMENT — SZPILMAN'S POINT OF VIEW — DAY

The interior of the Schutzpolizei building burnt to cinders.

An ambulance is being loaded with patients from the hospital.

A horse-drawn cab rounds a corner and clatters down the street.

INT./EXT. 2ND APARTMENT — SZPILMAN AND HIS POINT OF
VIEW — DAY

Szpilman at the window, watching.

The horse-drawn cab clatters out of his sight. He is about to draw back when he sees, directly beneath him, a man and woman walking with their hands in the air. Then, a German soldier, pointing his rifle at their backs, appears.

Suddenly, the man and woman begin to run.

The man turns and disappears. The woman also turns, but the German soldier drops to one knee and fires.

The woman clutches her stomach, drops slowly to her knees and collapses on the street in an awkward kneeling position, and that's how she remains.

Szpilman watches, aghast. Then, he hears voices outside his door, shouts, footsteps, panic.

The apartment:

He runs to his front door and listens.

> VOICES
> (*confused*)
> Where? Where? Just get out! Everywhere! Get out into the street!

More clatter of footsteps. Then:

> A MAN'S VOICE
> Get out now! The Germans have surrounded the building! They're going to blow us to pieces.

Footsteps descending stairs, more shouts, and:

> THE MAN'S VOICE
> (*further off*)
> Everyone out, please! Leave your flats at once, please!

Szpilman runs to the door, tries it but it's padlocked and he can't open the door.

In panic, he runs back to the window.

His eyes grow wide with terror.

Szpilman and his point of view: again the street.

A German tank bringing its gun to bear on the building next to his.

The gun jerks back and there's a great roaring noise.

The whole building shakes. Szpilman reels back, falls, gets to his feet and crawls back to the window.

He sees the tank turret swivelling slowly, bringing the gun to bear directly on a lower floor of his building. The roaring noise again.

A terrific explosion. His windows are shattered. Glass everywhere. He is thrown back across the room. Smoke begins to billow and fill the room.

INT. 2ND APARTMENT AND ADJOINING APARTMENT — DAY

Smoke filling the room. Szpilman gets to his knees, peers through the smoke and sees that the wall separating his apartment from the one next door has been partially destroyed, with a large hole blasted in it. He stumbles into the next-door apartment and out of the front door.

INT. 4TH AND 5TH FLOOR LANDINGS — DAY

Smoke everywhere. Szpilman staggers up to the fifth-floor landing. There's a metal attic door.

Szpilman pushes open the door and steps into the attic.

INT. ATTIC — DAY

The roof space with laundry drying on lines.

Szpilman enters the attic, closes the door, leans on it.

> GERMAN VOICE
> Fourth floor, Fischke!

He looks round, sees that the roof has been shattered, leaving a large, jagged gap. He climbs through the gap, on to the roof at the back of the building.

INT. 4TH FLOOR LANDING — DAY

The attic door being kicked in by a German boot.

A German soldier, wearing his gas mask, bayonet fixed, enters the attic, looks round, sees nothing, then:

GERMAN VOICE

At the double, Fischke!

The soldier turns and hurries out.

INT. ROOF, BACK OF BUILDING — DAY

On the sloping roof, Szpilman clutches the skylight and has his feet in the roof gutter.

He listens — all quiet in the house.

And then a bullet ricochets off the tiles beside him.

Szpilman, terrified, drops, involuntarily catching a lower edge so that his feet dangle above a balcony below. More shots. He drops on to the balcony and looks back.

EXT. ROOFTOP, TWO STREETS AWAY — DAY

Two German soldiers are firing at Szpilman.

INT. ROOF, BACK OF BUILDING — DAY

Szpilman clambers back into the building through the smashed balcony door. A couple of shots dangerously close.

INT. STAIRCASE — DAY

Smoke. Szpilman staggers down the stairs, stumbles over a corpse and almost falls headlong.

EXT. GARDEN AND BACKYARD — LATE AFTERNOON

The sun is setting.

Szpilman crawls into the backyard. He hears German voices shouting commands. He hides behind three garbage bins by the wall.

He waits. Listens. Silence.

EXT. STREET — EVENING

Deserted. Buildings on fire but dying out. Corpses in the street, including the woman who was shot, still in her strange kneeling position.

EXT. FRONT DOOR AND STREET — NIGHT

Szpilman watches from the doorway. Then, dropping down, he crawls across the road on his stomach, threading his way through the dead bodies, now besieged by flies, and makes for the hospital opposite.

German soldiers appear from around a corner. Szpilman immediately lies still, pretending to be just another corpse. Flies alight on him.

When the Germans pass, he sets off again.

INT. RUINED HOSPITAL, OPERATING THEATRE — NIGHT

Dark. Szpilman crawls into a corner, rests. He's exhausted.

He tries to take stock of his surroundings. He can make out the operating table. He manages to drag himself on to it.

He lies there, his eyes grow heavy. He sleeps.

EXT. RUINED HOSPITAL — DAY

German soldiers dragging the corpses into a pile.

A sergeant douses the bodies in petrol, then sets them alight.

The bodies burn.

INT./EXT. RUINED HOSPITAL — SZPILMAN AND HIS POINT OF VIEW — DAY

From a shattered window on the first floor, he looks at the burning bodies.

Two German soldiers wander into his eyeline. He draws back a little but watches them warily.

They sit just beneath him, chatting, and take out their food-tins, drink coffee and eat bread.

INT. PASSAGE AND WARDS, RUINED HOSPITAL — DAY

Szpilman wanders down the passage, sees into the wards, the empty beds, the broken furniture and medical equipment.

INT. KITCHEN, RUINED HOSPITAL — DAY

Szpilman opens cupboards, drawers, searching, but trying to be as quiet as possible.

He sees the refrigerator, quickly gets to it, pulls open the door. Empty.

He looks around and notices a red fire bucket with a spade and a box of sand next to it. The bucket is full of water, covered with an iridescent film and full of dead flies.

He drinks as much water as he can without swallowing the flies and, while he's doing so, he spots a couple of sacks.

He opens the first: potatoes. The second contains barley.

He tries to eat the uncooked barley but can't.

Later:

A fire on the floor. Szpilman holds a saucepan over it and is cooking the barley and some potatoes. He manages to scoop out a spoonful, blows to cool it, then eats.

INT./EXT. RUINED HOSPITAL — SZPILMAN AND HIS POINT OF VIEW — DAY

Szpilman at a window sees autumn leaves thick on the ground. And at the end of the street, a line of Poles, some with their hands in the air, others with hands on heads, being marched away by German soldiers.

INT. WARD. RUINED HOSPITAL — DAY.

Szpilman lies in bed under several layers of blankets. Ice on the windows. He hears German voices shouting commands. He sits up.

INT./EXT. RUINED HOSPITAL, SZPILMAN AND HIS POINT OF VIEW — DAY

Szpilman gets to a window and looks out.

German soldiers with flame-throwers are burning the buildings opposite.

One soldier, with a bucket of white paint and a brush, numbers the building.

Szpilman cranes to see them reach the end of the street, then cross over and start on the buildings on his side, working their way towards the hospital. He pulls away and makes for the back of the hospital.

INT. BACK OF RUINED HOSPITAL - DAY

Szpilman goes to a window, jumps out. He twists his ankle. He's in pain. He crawls across the back garden and climbs over the wall.

EXT. RUINED STREETS — DAY

Devastation, not a human being in sight.

Nothing. Emptiness.

He is alone.

Szpilman hobbles away.

EXT. RUINED VILLA — EVENING

Cautiously, Szpilman limps towards the villa, a once grand building, but now partly damaged by shell fire.

He makes his way in.

INT. HALL, RUINED VILLA — EVENING

Szpilman enters the hall, still showing signs of its former opulence. Silent. Ominous.

He looks round anxiously, then sees the stairs leading down to the basement. He hurries towards them and descends.

INT. KITCHEN, RUINED VILLA — EVENING

Dark, shadowy.

Szpilman comes down a flight of wooden stairs that lead directly into the kitchen.

Immediately, he begins to search frantically, opening cupboards, drawers. He finds a can with a label illustrating pickled cucumbers. Desperately, he searches for something to open it with.

He discovers a pair of scales with a variety of weights. He seizes one of the weights when, very close, he hears the sound of a car coming to a halt, then the car door slam, a German voice giving commands.

He drops the weight but, holding the tin, he scampers up the stairs.

INT. BACK STAIRS, RUINED VILLA — EVENING

Szpilman, clutching the unopened tin, makes his way up the narrow, wooden staircase.

INT. TOP FLOOR, RUINED VILLA — EVENING

Szpilman, panting heavily, reaches the top floor.

He sees a small door, tries it. It opens.

INT. ATTIC AND LOFT, RUINED VILLA — EVENING

Szpilman enters, closing the small door behind him. He leans back, resting, recovering.

And then he hears from down below a piano playing a Beethoven piece.

After a few bars, the music stops. Szpilman listens anxiously. Silence.

He looks around, finding himself in an attic space filled with junk, a ladder, rotting material, travelling trunks. Last light of day filtering through a dormer window.

There's a ladder leading up to a trapdoor. Szpilman climbs the ladder.

He crawls into a small empty space. With enormous effort he pulls up the ladder and closes the trapdoor.

Exhausted and trying to catch his breath, he gazes at the unopened tin. He peers through the darkness but sees nothing.

His eyes begin to droop.

EXT. WARSAW CITY SKYLINE — NIGHT

Artillery fire. Fires glow on the horizon.

INT. LOFT, RUINED VILLA — NIGHT

Szpilman wakes suddenly. He listens. Silence but for the distant gunfire. He sees the unopened tin of pickles, stares at it. He opens the trapdoor.

INT. BACK STAIRS, RUINED VILLA — NIGHT

Szpilman, a shadow, a spectre, creeps down the stairs.

INT. KITCHEN, RUINED VILLA — NIGHT

Szpilman has placed the tin and the weight on a shelf and is engrossed in searching again. He finds a pair of chicken scissors. Using the weight, he starts to hammer the point of the scissors into the tin making a perforation round the rim.

The tin slips off the shelf and rolls across the floor coming to rest at a pair of highly polished jackboots. Szpilman stifles a gasp.

On the stairs, in silhouette, gazing down at him, the figure of a German Captain, the thumb of one hand caught in his belt above his pistol.

THE GERMAN CAPTAIN
(*stern*)

Who the hell are you?

Szpilman just stares at him.

Who are you?

No response.

What the hell are you doing?

SZPILMAN
(*barely audible, in German*)
I was – I was trying to open this tin –

THE GERMAN CAPTAIN
Where do you live?

No response.

What's your work?

SZPILMAN
I am – I was a pianist.

THE GERMAN CAPTAIN
A pianist.

He studies Szpilman for a moment, then with a nod orders him to follow. Szpilman picks up the tin and follows.

INT. ROOMS, RUINED VILLA – NIGHT

Szpilman follows the German Captain through a double door, hanging off its hinges, into a room with a broken table in the centre, what once was the dining room. And then through another set of doors. The German Captain's boots echo.

They come into a spacious room. Faint moonlight filters through the large windows. Fallen masonry and broken glass. A couple of chairs. And a grand piano in the corner.

The German Captain points at the piano.

THE GERMAN CAPTAIN
      Play.

Szpilman hesitates, then limps to the piano, puts down the tin, and opens the lid. He turns and drags one of the chairs over and sits.

The German Captain stands and watches.

Szpilman glances surreptitiously at his hands, and then he plays Chopin.

The German Captain listens, expressionless. The pale moonlight shows him to be a handsome, elegant man.

Szpilman finishes playing.

Silence.

Somewhere, a cat mews. Distant burst of rifle fire.

The German Captain stares at Szpilman. After a moment:

THE GERMAN CAPTAIN
      Are you hiding here?

Szpilman nods.

      Jew?

Long pause. Szpilman just stares at him.

      Where are you hiding?

SZPILMAN
(*in German*)
      In the attic.

THE GERMAN CAPTAIN
      Show me.

Szpilman hesitates, takes the tin and then shuffles past the German Captain towards the door.

INT. ATTIC AND LOFT AREA, RUINED VILLA — NIGHT

Szpilman and the German Captain enter.

The German Captain takes out a flashlight, sees the ladder in place, leading up to the loft.

Szpilman climbs the ladder, squeezes into the loft and looks down at the German Captain, who shines his light on him.

THE GERMAN CAPTAIN
Have you anything to eat?

Szpilman shows him the tin.

I'll bring you something.

He goes quickly, leaving Szpilman in darkness.

Szpilman, overcome by relief, can barely catch his breath.

EXT. RUINED VILLA — NIGHT

The German Captain strides out of the villa, down the front steps to a waiting car and a driver. He gets into the car. The driver starts the engine and the car speeds off into the night.

INT. LOFT — NIGHT

Szpilman hears the car's engine growing fainter. He starts to tremble and then begins to cry. He weeps uncontrollably.

INT. HALL, ROOMS, RUINED VILLA — DAY

Much activity: officers coming and going, orderlies typing. Officers talking on field telephones. Desks, filing cabinets.

The German Captain, carrying a bulging shoulder bag, marches into a room just off the hall and goes to his desk just as an orderly drops papers in his in-tray. On the desk, there's a framed photograph of him with a woman and two children.

The German Captain glances at the papers, takes a pen, initials one or two and then goes.

The grand staircase:

The German Captain marches up the stairs purposefully, as if he's on urgent business.

INT. LOFT AND ATTIC — DAY

The German Captain enters. He puts two fingers in his mouth and whistles.

> THE GERMAN CAPTAIN
> Open up.

After a moment, the trapdoor shifts and Szpilman looks down.

The German Captain takes a package from his shoulder bag and throws it up into the loft. He turns to go.

> SZPILMAN
> Please —

The German Captain stops.

> What's all that gunfire?

> THE GERMAN CAPTAIN
> The Russians. On the other side of the river.

Turns to leave, stops; with a touch of irony:

> All you have to do is hang on for a few more weeks.

He goes quickly.

Szpilman opens the package, finds bread and marmalade. Then he finds a tin-opener.

EXT. RUINED VILLA — DAY

Snow. The sound of distant gunfire.

The Germans are evacuating the villa. Men carry out boxes, filing cabinets, desks, papers and load them into trucks. They're careless, leaving a trail of debris. No sentries now.

INT. ATTIC AND LOFT AREA, RUINED VILLA — DAY

Szpilman, listening and shivering with cold. He hears the whistle. He opens the trapdoor to see the German Captain in the attic, carrying a package.

> THE GERMAN CAPTAIN

Come down.

Szpilman descends.

> SZPILMAN

What's happening?

> THE GERMAN CAPTAIN

We're getting out.

Szpilman faces the German Captain.

> SZPILMAN
> (*in German*)

Are the Russians here?

> THE GERMAN CAPTAIN

Not yet.

He hands Szpilman the package. Szpilman opens it to find inside several loaves of bread.

> SZPILMAN

I don't know how to thank you.

> THE GERMAN CAPTAIN

Don't thank me. Thank God. It's His will that we should survive. Well. That's what we have to believe.

Silence. Szpilman shivers with cold. The German Captain takes off his coat and gives it to him.

> SZPILMAN

What about you?

> THE GERMAN CAPTAIN

I've got another one. Warmer.

Brief pause.

What will you do when it's all over?

> SZPILMAN
> I'll play the piano again. On Polish radio.

> THE GERMAN CAPTAIN
> Tell me your name. I'll listen out for you.

> SZPILMAN
> Szpilman.

> THE GERMAN CAPTAIN
> Szpilman. (*a crooked smile*) Good name for a pianist.

EXT. STREETS NEAR RUINED VILLA — DAY

Freezing weather.

Empty streets.

Then the sound of recorded music, as a car, with a loudspeaker and a Polish national flag, comes into view, the Polish national anthem blaring out from the speaker.

INT. LOFT — DAY

Szpilman, wearing the German Captain's coat and under the eiderdown, hears the strange sound of the music, which he recognises.

He's astonished, puzzled. He comes to a decision and starts to leave.

INT./EXT. HALL AND STREET, RUINED VILLA — DAY

Cautiously, in his German military overcoat, Szpilman trots down the staircase into the empty hall.

He goes to the front door, opens it a crack and cautiously goes out.

EXT. STREET — DAY

Szpilman looks around, hearing the car loudspeaker indistinctly.

– German army – Polish soil liberated – official –

His excitement grows and he walks out into the street.

He sees at one end soldiers serving soup from a field kitchen to a group of people.

On the opposite side of the street, he sees a man and a woman who have left the field kitchen. The man carries a two-tiered canister.

Szpilman rushes towards them, grabs hold of the man and tries to kiss him. The man, totally bewildered, tries to fight him off. The woman is terrified.

THE WOMAN
German! German!

She runs, yelling, towards the field kitchen. So does the man.

Szpilman stands and stares, then sees one of the soldiers cock his rifle and fire at him.

Szpilman runs, the firing continuing.

EXT. RUINS – DAY

Szpilman bolts into the doorway of a ruined building. He peers out to see Polish soldiers beginning to surround the ruined building, firing shots, lobbing in a grenade or two.

SZPILMAN
(shouting)
Stop, for God's sake, I beg you, I'm Polish!

More shots and another grenade explosion.

Don't shoot! I'm Polish!

The Polish soldiers:

Two of the officers stand near the entrance, hearing Szpilman's shouts.

1ST POLISH OFFICER
He's Polish –

> 2ND POLISH OFFICER
> (*yelling*)
Come out with your hands up.

> SZPILMAN
> (*obeying*)
Don't shoot! I'm Polish! Please, please! I'm Polish!

> 1ST POLISH OFFICER
Yes, he's Polish –

> 2ND POLISH OFFICER
> (*as Szpilman approaches*)
Why the fucking coat?

> SZPILMAN
I'm cold –

The Polish officers confer briefly in whispers. Then:

> 2ND POLISH OFFICER
Take him to headquarters.

And they march him off.

EXT. LONG COUNTRY LANE AND HOLDING CAMP – DAY

Spring. Idyllic.

A column of men and women stretching along the length of the lane. A couple of horse-and-carts. One or two bicycles. Some of the people wear concentration camp garb, others in tattered clothing.

Four men walk together and when they come to a narrow junction, stop, seeing something.

Behind barbed wire, German prisoners of war, guarded by Russian soldiers. Desolate place. No shelters, no tents. The POWs sit or lie on the ground, silent, broken, shattered.

The four men gaze at them.

> 1ST MAN
Look at them – bastards.

2ND MAN

German fuckers –

3RD MAN

I prayed for this, never thought I'd see it –

The fourth man, Zygmunt Lednicki, approaches the barbed wire.

LEDNICKI

Murderers! Assassins! Look at you now! You took
everything I had! Me, a musician! (*wagging his finger
fiercely*) You took my violin! You took my soul!

*He stands glowering at them, then sees a POW rise from a group,
wretched, shabby, unshaven. It's the German Captain, uniform
tattered, a wreck. He comes to the barbed wire.*

THE GERMAN CAPTAIN
(*urgent*)
(*in German*)

Do you happen to know another musician, a Mr Szpilman?
A pianist! Polish radio –

LEDNICKI

Yes, of course, I know Szpilman.

THE GERMAN CAPTAIN
(*desperate*)

I helped Mr Szpilman when he was in hiding. Tell him I'm
here. Ask him to help me –

*A Russian guard, inside the compound, approaches, grabs hold of the
German Captain.*

RUSSIAN GUARD
(*to Lednicki, in Russian*)

Hey! No talking to the prisoners. Get away from there –

He drags the German Captain away from the wire.

LEDNICKI
(*as he backs away, calling*)

What's your name?

The German Captain is being bundled away by the guard, who aims a kick at him. The German Captain shouts out his name but it's unintelligible.

LEDNICKI

What?

The German Captain and the guard have disappeared. Lednicki stands for a moment, then turns and goes.

INT. STUDIO, WARSAW RADIO STATION — DAY

Szpilman playing the piano. He looks something like his former self, fairly well dressed and groomed.

He glances towards the glass booth and sees Lednicki with the technicians. He smiles. Lednicki nods, smiles back.

EXT. SITE OF POW CAMP — DAY

Szpilman and Lednicki looking around an empty field.

LEDNICKI

It was here, I'm certain of it –

SZPILMAN

It's not here now.

LEDNICKI

I shouted abuse at them, I'm not proud of it, but that's what I did, and, I'm certain, I stood where you are now. There was barbed wire, and this German came up to me.

SZPILMAN

You didn't catch his name.

LEDNICKI

No. I'll ask at the factory. They may know something.

Lednicki goes.

Szpilman stands, looking around the empty field. He is filled with sadness. He sits. He closes his eyes and put his face to the sun.

Superimpose caption:

IT WAS LATER DISCOVERED THAT
THE NAME OF THE GERMAN OFFICER
WAS CAPTAIN WILM HOSENFELD.
ALL THAT IS KNOWN IS THAT HE DIED IN
A SOVIET PRISONER-OF-WAR CAMP IN 1952.
WLADYSLAW SZPILMAN CONTINUED TO LIVE
IN WARSAW UNTIL HIS DEATH ON 6 JULY 2000.
HE WAS EIGHTY-EIGHT YEARS OLD.

INT. CONCERT HALL – NIGHT

Szpilman plays Chopin's Piano Concerto No 1 with full orchestra and conductor. He plays superbly. The music is glorious.

Fade out.

Taking Sides

adapted from the play by
Ronald Harwood

CAST AND CREW

MAIN CAST

MAJOR STEVE ARNOLD	Harvey Keitel
LIEUTENANT DAVID WILLS	Moritz Bleibtreu
DR WILHELM FURTWÄNGLER	Stellan Skarsgård
EMMI STRAUBE	Birgit Minichmayr
HELMUTH RODE	Ulrich Tukur
COLONEL DYMSHITZ	Oleg Tabakov
RUDOLF WERNER	Hans Zischler
SCHLEE	Armin Rohde
GENERAL WALLACE	R. Lee Ermey
CAPTAIN ED MARTIN	August Zirner
SERGEANT ADAMS	Daniel White
REICHSMINISTER	Thomas Thieme
COLONEL GREEN	Jed Curtis
MAJOR RICHARDS	Garrick Hagon
CAPTAIN VERNAY	Robin Renucci
ATTENDANT	Markus Heinicke
PROJECTIONIST	Aleksander Tesla
US SOLDIER	Jarreth J. Merz
STEVE'S DRIVER	Holger Schober
FRENCH AIDE	Frank Leboeuf
US AIDE	Philip Bowen
BRITISH SERGEANT	Thomas Morris
BRITISH OFFICER	Peter Doering
JAZZ SINGER	Rinat Shaham
REMER	Werner Armeln
SCHMIDT	Matthias Wilke
AIDE 1	Holger Jahn
AIDE 2	Werner Zwosta
BARKEEPER 1	Thomas Rösicke
BARKEEPER 2	Marco Riccardi
RUSSIAN AIDE	Jourii Babalikachvili
UK AIDE	Henry Schindler
US SOLDIER	Chris Martin
STALLHOLDER	Benno Wirth
BOY 1	Ron Hermann
BOY 2	Valentin Tornow

MAIN CREW

Director	István Szabó
Screenplay	Ronald Harwood
Co-Executive Producer	Fritz Buttenstedt
Co-Producers	Jeremy Isaacs, Maureen McCabe,
	Rainer Mockert, Jaques Rousseau
	Rainer Schaper,
	Michael von Wolkenstein
Producer	Yves Pasquier
Line Producer	Udo Happel
Supervising Producer	Michel Nicolini
Associate Producer	Gisela Waetzoldt
Cinematography	Lajos Koltai
Editor	Sylvie Landra
Production Design	Ken Adam

Fade in:

INT. BERLIN CONCERT HALL (1944) — NIGHT

A man conducting Beethoven. Air raid in progress. Bombs falling nearby. The orchestra continues to play. Suddenly the lights go out. The music stops.

INT. BACKSTAGE CORRIDOR, CONCERT HALL — NIGHT

A beam from a torch, bouncing, making shadows. An attendant, carrying the torch, hurries down the corridor. The air raid continues.

He comes to a door, knocks, opens it and looks in.

> ATTENDANT
> (*agitated*)
> Dr Furtwängler, the Reichsminister –

The sound of heavy footsteps approaching. The attendant turns his torch to light the way for three men in Nazi uniform, also with attendants and torches, marching down the corridor.

The attendant bows deeply as the Reichsminister and his aide go through the door. The other man remains in the corridor on guard.

INT. CONDUCTOR'S ROOM — NIGHT

Candles light the room where the conductor shakes hands with the Reichsminister.

> REICHSMINISTER
> Dr Furtwängler, I want to apologise personally for this power failure. I was so enjoying the performance. In times like these we need spiritual nourishment.

A bomb explodes nearby.

But I welcome this unexpected opportunity of talking to you. (*with great care*) When you came on to the platform tonight, I thought you weren't well. You looked tired. (*a warning*) Get away from this bombing. Away from the war. Yes, you look tired – (*a crooked smile*) – even in this light –

INT. RUINED CINEMA — DAY

Dark. On a screen: scenes from Leni Riefenstahl's Triumph of the Will. *Over this:*

A MAN'S VOICE

Look at them. Men, women, kids. Boy, did they love him. You see, Steve, Adolf Hitler touched something deep, real deep and savage and barbaric, and it won't just go away overnight. It's got to be rooted out. You know what I think? I think they were all Nazis. And let's face it, their leaders, those bastards now on trial in Nuremberg, couldn't have done it alone. It's these people, they gave all the help that was needed. Willingly.

The film changes with a scratchy music soundtrack – Wagner. Shots of high-ranking Nazis in an audience including Josef Goebbels, listening. And they're listening to and watching Wilhelm Furtwängler conducting. At the appropriate moment:

THE MAN'S VOICE

That's him. Furtwängler. Wilhelm Furtwängler.

The Nazis applaud. Goebbels shakes hands with Furtwängler. The film ends.

Sitting in the ruined cinema are two men: General Wallace, with files on the table, and, beside him, Major Steve Arnold. A projectionist is standing in the door of the projection room.

WALLACE

So, you never heard of him.

STEVE

Nope.

WALLACE

Do you know who Arturo Toscanini is?

STEVE

Sure.

WALLACE

He's as big as Toscanini, maybe even bigger. In this neck of the woods, he's probably Bob Hope and Betty Grable rolled into one.

STEVE

Jeez, and I never heard of him.

Wallace glances at the file.

WALLACE

You were in insurance before the war.

STEVE

Right. Claims assessor.

WALLACE

Conscientious, determined, dogged.

STEVE
(*amused*)

They said I was dogged?

WALLACE

Well, they say here that when you went on a case, you stayed on it. (*Looks up at Steve.*) Now we can't take every Nazi in this country to trial, although I would like to; it's an impossibility. So we're going for the big boys in industry, education, law, culture –

STEVE

Like this bandleader –

WALLACE
(*a smile*)

Well, he's more than just a bandleader, Steve. He's a great conductor, a gifted artist. But we believe that he sold himself to the devil. Your number one priority from this moment on is to connect him to the Nazi Party. Don't be impressed by him. I want the folks back home to understand why we fought this war. Find Wilhelm Furtwängler guilty. He represents everything that was rotten in Germany.

Steve wants to rise, but Wallace puts a hand on his shoulder to make him sit again.

Stay put, Steve. There is some other stuff that I'd like for you to see here. Background.

He nods to the projectionist, then starts to go, but stops.

Oh, one thing that may be a problem. Our Occupation Authorities in Wiesbaden have a duty to help these poor unfortunates with their defence. They keep repeating: 'We must be just, we must be seen to be just.' Well, I've only one thing to say to the liberals in Wiesbaden: fuck 'em. (*as he goes*) You answer to no one but me. Is that understood? (*to the projectionist in the door*) Show him the film.

PROJECTIONIST

Yes, sir. Roll it.

Wallace goes. The projectionist starts the next reel.

On the screen: a Berlin sequence. Bombs falling. Ruins, a city devastated, empty. Flags of the four Allied nations. Posters of Truman, Stalin, Churchill.

ARCHIVE FILM VOICE

That is the hand that dropped the bombs on defenceless Rotterdam, Brussels, Belgrade. That is the hand that destroyed the cities, villages and homes of Russia. That is the hand that held the whip over the Polish, Yugoslav, French and Norwegian slaves. That is the hand that took their food.

Steve watches expressionless.

STEVE

Next reel, please.

On the screen: shots of camp survivors. Then shots of emaciated corpses being bulldozed into mass graves.

ARCHIVE FILM

Sanitary conditions were so appalling that heavy equipment had to be brought in to speed the work of cleaning up. This was Bergen Belsen.

The moment this appears, Steve rises and goes quickly.

On the screen: piles of cadavers.

INT. MAJOR STEVE ARNOLD'S BEDROOM (1945) — NIGHT

Steve having a nightmare, twisting, turning, moaning. He wakes with a cry. He is sweating. He turns on the light, looks at a clock, reaches for a cigarette, lights it. He smokes. He stares at the ceiling.

Later:

Early morning. Cold. Steve is at the basin in his small room, shaving. A radio on a shelf.

AMERICAN RADIO VOICE

Remember, men, no fraternisation. In a German town, if you bow to a pretty girl or pat a blond child, you bow to all that Hitler stood for. You bow to his reign of blood. You caress the ideology that meant death and destruction. You never know who was a member of the Nazi Party. Don't be fooled. Don't fraternise.

EXT. STEVE'S OFFICE BUILDING, BERLIN — DAY

Steve's car swerves round the corner and comes to a halt. A small crowd watch workmen on ladders hammering away at a stone swastika above the portico. American soldiers supervise. Steve gets out of the car, carrying an attaché case, and he, too, watches as the stone swastika falls and crashes into pieces on the road. One or two people clap, most just stare.

The American soldiers immediately hoist the Stars and Stripes. Steve goes into the building. The sentry salutes.

The driver of the car goes to the trunk and takes out a labelled duffel bag, cans of film, a case which holds a 16-mm projector. A small boy sidles up to him:

> BOY
>
> Cigarettes, chewing gum?

INT. WAITING ROOM — DAY

Steve and Sergeant Adams ascending a grand, winding but damaged staircase to the rear of a spacious entrance hall. A once impressive building. Signs of bomb damage everywhere. German workmen doing repairs. American military personnel coming and going, saluting Steve, who barely acknowledges them.

They reach the landing. Adams opens double doors and they go through.

> ADAMS
>
> We're gonna have the heating fixed by tonight.

A few gilt chairs, a workman trying to repair the stove. Adams opens another door for Steve.

INT. STEVE'S OFFICE — DAY

Emmi is hanging the standard photograph of President Truman on the wall. She turns to see Steve and Adams and is covered with confusion. She gives Steve a little curtsey.

> ADAMS
>
> Fräulein, this is Major Arnold. Sir, this is your secretary, Fräulein Emmi Straube. Her file's on your desk. They sent her over from Admin. I'll leave you to it.

He goes. Steve scrutinises Emmi. She's embarrassed, keeps her eyes downcast. Steve goes to his desk, opens a file, reads.

> STEVE
>
> You live here, in Berlin?

> EMMI
>
> Yes.

STEVE

You do shorthand and typing?

EMMI

Yes.

He nods, goes on reading.

STEVE

Okay, let's see. How long were you in the camp for?

EMMI

Three months.

STEVE

Says here because of your father. What's that mean?

EMMI

My father was one of the officers in the plot against Hitler.
They arrested the plotters and their families.

STEVE

Your mother, too.

EMMI

Yes. She suffered longer. She was in Ravensbruck.

STEVE

And your father was executed.

She nods, keeps her eyes averted. He smiles sympathetically.

STEVE

I'm gonna call you Emmi, you're gonna call me Steve.
Okay?

No response.

I got a list of stuff here I'd like you to get for me.

He searches his pockets.

ADAMS

If you need anything, let me know.

EMMI

Major –

Steve –

EMMI

There have been messages for you. (*She consults the pad.*)
A Lieutenant David Wills called from the Allied Kommandatura Cultural Affairs office in Wiesbaden. I don't know
who he is.

Steve starts to unpack his attaché case.

Then there have been three calls from Dr Furtwängler
wanting to know when you wish to see him. I did not speak
to him personally . . .

*She hands Steve a typewritten sheet. He ignores it, finds a list which
he hands to her. He waits for her to read, then:*

STEVE

Think you can get me any of that?

EMMI
(*pleased*)

Oh yes, Major, I have recordings of all his symphonies.
I kept them safe during the bombing. My favourite is the
Seventh Symphony.

STEVE

Mine's the Eleventh.

EMMI
(*puzzled*)

But – he only wrote nine, Major.

STEVE

I'm kidding, Emmi. What about a record player? You have
that, too?

EMMI

No. Ours was damaged.

STEVE
(*surveys the room*)

What's in those files?

EMMI

The names of the members of the Berlin Philharmonic
Orchestra since 1934 together with their questionnaires.
Major – what am I to tell Dr Furtwängler?

STEVE

You tell him nothing, Emmi. If he calls again, you say you
know nothing. We're gonna keep him waiting while I get
acquainted with his case and with the witnesses. And, God
help me, with Beethoven.

He smiles. She tries to smile back.

EXT. FLEA MARKET, BERLIN – DAY

*Freezing weather. A narrow street, crowded, busy, noisy. Some makeshift
stalls set out, trestle tables, open suitcases, people buying and selling
every imaginable commodity.*

*Emmi wanders through the crowd, passing a violinist, Helmuth Rode,
wrapped up against the cold, playing Handel's Air on a G String,
a bowl for money at his feet. A passer-by drops a cigarette butt in it.
Immediately, Rode retrieves the butt.*

*Emmi comes to a stall selling piles of gramophone records. She asks the
stallholder a question. He points to another stall across the way.*

INT. STEVE'S OFFICE – DAY

Steve at his desk, paging through files. A knock on the door.

STEVE

Yeah –

*Lieutenant David Wills, aged twenty-four, enters, comes to Steve's
desk, stands to attention, salutes.*

DAVID

Lieutenant Wills reporting to Major Arnold. Sir.

STEVE

For Chrissakes I hate that shit, cut it out.

DAVID

I'm very sorry.

STEVE

I'm Steve. What's your name?

DAVID

David. David Wills. I'm your liaison officer with the Allied
Kommandatura Cultural Affairs Committee. Sir.

STEVE

Sounds a lot of fun. (*Studies David.*) So they sent the big
guns to check up on me. We recruiting children now?

DAVID
(*smiles*)

I guess so, sir.

STEVE

You call me sir again and I'll make you listen to Beethoven.

David half-smiles.

Where you from, David?

DAVID

I was born here, in Leipzig. I escaped in '36. My parents,
they sent me to my uncle in Philadelphia. They were to
follow. But they delayed and –

Breaks off. Nothing from Steve.

Our family name was Weill. But that doesn't sound well in
English. My uncle changed it to Wills and –

*The door opens and Emmi enters carrying a record player, sees David
and starts to back out.*

EMMI

I'm sorry –

STEVE

Come in, Emmi, this is your office, too. Emmi, this is
Lieutenant David Wills.

They nod briefly.

He is here to watch over us.

A flick from Emmi.

> STEVE
>
> I guess you admire musicians.

> DAVID
>
> Some.

> STEVE
>
> Don't. This is like a criminal investigation, David.
> Musicians, morticians, doctors, lawyers, butchers, clerks.
> They're all the same.

For Emmi's benefit too. She becomes still, listens.

We have a duty, a moral duty.

David takes a few files, sits and starts to look through them. Steve returns to his files. Emmi, by now, has put on a record and starts to play it: the opening of Beethoven's Fifth Symphony blasts out.

The two men look up, startled. Emmi beams:

> EMMI
>
> It works!

> STEVE
>
> Hallelujah!

INT. STEVE'S OFFICE – DAY

Emmi at the door. Steve at his desk. David present.

> EMMI
>
> Herr Rudolf Werner.

Werner enters, bows to Steve and David. Emmi goes to her desk.

> STEVE
>
> Sit down, Werner.

Indicates the upright chair; Werner sits.

I want you to understand why you're here. This is an investigation into Wilhelm Furtwängler, former Prussian Privy Councillor, banned from public life under Control Council Directive No 24 and who's applied to come before the Tribunal of Artists of the Denazification Commission. I'm interested in what he was up to from 1933 to the end of the war, understood?

Werner nods.

> STEVE

Rudolf Otto Werner. Wind section since 1936. What instrument did you play?

> WERNER

First oboe.

> STEVE

I have your questionnaire here. It says you were never a member of the Nazi Party.

> WERNER

Absolutely not.

Long silence; Steve watches him. Werner is made more anxious. At last, in a rush:

> WERNER

No, I was never a Nazi, I have no interest in politics, I'm a musician –

> STEVE

Hey, hey, slow up, Fräulein Straube has to take down what you say –

Werner swivels round to look at Emmi.

> WERNER

Straube? Any relation to Colonel Joachim Straube?

> EMMI

My father.

> WERNER

It's a great honour to meet you, Fräulein. Your father was a great patriot.

Brief silence.

Dr Furtwängler is a great musician. He actively opposed the Nazis and later on he helped many Jews to escape.

> STEVE

Then how do you explain him being made a Prussian Privy Councillor?

> WERNER

It was Hermann Goering. I was told he just made the maestro his Privy Councillor, no questions asked. Although Dr Furtwängler stood up to him. And to Dr Goebbels.

> STEVE

He also conducted for Hitler, didn't he?

> WERNER

Yes, that's true, but he refused to give the Nazi salute. He kept his baton in his right hand. In Hitler's presence. That was a brave act –

> STEVE

Brave? To celebrate Hitler's birthday with some heroic piece by Wagner but without the Nazi salute? Bravo.

> WERNER

It was Beethoven's Ninth.

> STEVE

Do you really think it was brave? Didn't he bow to him and shake his hand?

INT. STEVE'S OFFICE – DAY

Another man, Schlee, is in the chair. Only Steve and Emmi now. Pale, yellow electric light. Silence. Schlee, too, is very nervous. At last:

> SCHLEE

No, no, no, I give you my word. I was never a member of the Nazi Party. Never. I am in the percussion section. I play the timpani.

Steve just stares at him.

Anyway, they would never have allowed it. My brother was married to a Jewess, may she rest in peace. And Goebbels said – (*to Emmi*) – please take this down carefully, because it's most important, Fräulein –?

EMMI

Straube.

SCHLEE
(acting surprised)

Straube? Are you by any chance related to Colonel Joachim Straube?

EMMI

My father.

SCHLEE

He was – he was a great hero.

Steve lights a cigarette.

Goebbels, yes, Josef Goebbels said, 'There's not a single filthy Jew left in Germany on whose behalf Dr Furtwängler has not intervened.' No, no one could have been less of a Nazi than Dr Furtwängler.

STEVE

But this was the same guy who conducted for Adolf on his birthday –

SCHLEE

He was forced to do that. But he refused to give the Nazi salute in front of Hitler. He kept his baton in his hand, you can't salute with a baton in your hand.

DAVID

And what about the Nuremberg Rally?

SCHLEE

No, we – we played on the evening before the Rally.

STEVE
(straight-faced)

Oh! The evening before, I see –

134

SCHLEE

Yes, Dr Furtwängler was absolutely clear about this: politics
and art must be kept separate –

STEVE

Politics and art must be kept separate. I'll remember that.
But let me see if you can help me with something I just
don't understand. I'd really like to know why all you guys
are so crazy about him. What's his secret?

Schlee tries to find words.

SCHLEE

Well, it's hard to explain. I can only tell you from my own
experience. Soon after I joined the orchestra, we were
rehearsing the Third Symphony of Beethoven, the Eroica.
There are several rather difficult passages for the timpani.
One particular crescendo. During the break, I asked how he
wanted it played. He was studying his score. He didn't look
up. He said, 'Just watch me.' So, of course, I did. I never
stopped watching him. The moment came. And suddenly, he
turned to me and our eyes were locked. There was something
in his look that – that simply demanded the crescendo.
I shall never forget his look. It was a moment of – of magic.

Steve nods, thinks for a moment. Then:

STEVE

You ever seen Adolf Hitler's eyes when he was making a
speech? I've seen 'em on films.

SCHLEE

Yes.

STEVE

Was looking at Furtwängler like that?

SCHLEE

I don't know what you mean, Major.

STEVE

When you got to the crescendo.

Schlee looks at him bewildered.

INT./EXT. CAR (TRAVELLING), LAKESIDE AND MANSION — DAY

*In the back, David and Steve. Military driver. The car's making its
way along a road that skirts a lake towards a grand mansion from
which fly the four Allied flags.*

STEVE

You think a whole orchestra, what, a hundred and forty or
so guys, could be orchestrated?

DAVID

I guess it's possible.

STEVE

So, what does the Russki want?

DAVID

Colonel Dymshitz asked specially to see you.

STEVE

'Dim-shits'?

INT. THE MANSION — DAY

A huge, cavernous room, once the ballroom.

*In the centre, a table with four chairs. To one side, antique furniture,
objets d'art, paintings. Four Allied officers are surveying the treasures:
Colonel Dymshitz, Colonel Green (American), Major Richards (British)
and Captain Vernay (French). What they say is barely audible, low
mumbles. They're accompanied by aides with clipboards, taking notes.*

*Beyond, and some distance away, a row of gilt chairs for observers
where David and Steve take their seats.*

STEVE

What the hell are they doing?

DAVID
(*whispered*)

They're trying to sort out some of the works of art the
Nazis stole from occupied territories. Who really owns
what? That's Colonel Dymshitz, on the far side –

Dymshitz, small, intelligent face, cunning eyes.

136

> DAVID'S VOICE
> – art historian, head of the famous Leningrad Museum of
> Art. He is an expert on German culture.

Green, correct, formal, precise, immaculate.

Richards, bespectacled and nondescript.

Vernay, upright, proud.

> VERNAY
> (*suddenly raising his voice*)
> *Je suis navré, Colonel, cette peinture n'est pas la propriété de
> l'union soviétique mais bien celle de la France.*

> GREEN
> What's he saying? Henri, what is you saying? –

> AMERICAN AIDE
> He saying that picture is the property of France –

> VERNAY
> *C'est un Braque qui avec Picasso était un des pionniers du
> cubisme.*

> DYMSHITZ
> (*in French*)
> I know who Georges Braque is, Captain –

> AMERICAN AIDE
> (*almost simultaneously*)
> It's a Braque.

> FRENCH AIDE
> We can produce the provenance of this Braque, you say
> provenance –?

INT./EXT. SALON OFF THE BALLROOM AND TERRACE – DAY

*Outside the club room for the participants. Buzz of conversation, clink
of glasses, cups. The terrace is deserted.*

*A waiter carries a tray with various refreshments to a quiet corner
where Dymshitz, Green, Vernay, his aide Lieutenant Simon, Steve and*

David sit in comfortable armchairs. The waiter serves them. During this:

DYMSHITZ

Hello, Major, my name is Dymshitz. I'm glad to see you.

STEVE

Colonel. Pleasure.

DYMSHITZ

So, Major, tell me, have you questioned Dr Furtwängler?

STEVE

Not yet.

DYMSHITZ

I've had two meetings with him. He's a great musician. Maybe the greatest conductor in the world. His Brahms, Beethoven, Schubert – unequalled.

Steve makes a non-committal gesture.

I'll come straight to point. I've offered him a very attractive position. Conductor of the Staatsoper Unten den Linden. He refused. But I want him. I want him badly. And I want your help.

GREEN

Hey, just a moment, you should have discussed this with me first –

DYMSHITZ

I'm discussing it with you now. Major, I want you to drop your investigation, save everybody time and trouble –

GREEN

We can't drop a case just like that –

DYMSHITZ

I'll give you another conductor in exchange or writer, musician, actor what – what do you care? But I like Furtwängler. He's my favourite conductor. (*Chuckles.*) Mine and Hitler's. He's our favourite conductor.

INT. WAITING ROOM — DAY

Rode is seated, waiting. Nervous, tense. The sound of laughter, David's laughter from the office. It makes him even more uncomfortable.

INT. STEVE'S OFFICE SUITE — DAY

Emmi and David laughing.

> DAVID
>
> I clicked my heels, saluted and bowed at the same time.

He demonstrates. She laughs again.

> EMMI
>
> That's because you had a proper upbringing.

> DAVID
>
> That's right. I was raised very strictly. So don't speak before you are spoken to!

> EMMI
>
> Oh! And don't wave your hands about!

> DAVID
>
> Respect your elders and your betters!

> EMMI
>
> And no elbows on the table!

> DAVID
>
> Eating is eating – and –

> EMMI
>
> And talking is talking! Well, I think we better get on –

> DAVID
>
> Right. So, this is going to be very formal, too, now.
> Lieutenant David Wills requests the pleasure of the company of Fräulein Emmi Straube at dinner any night she cares –

She smiles just as Steve bursts in. He's in a bright, cheerful, energetic mood.

David draws back guiltily. Emmi, embarrassed, hesitates then turns to the typewriter and types furiously. Seeing this, Steve stops, but just for a brief moment. Then, as he goes to his desk:

STEVE

David, need to ask you something. You heard this rumour the British found something called the Hinkel Archive?

DAVID

Yes.

STEVE

So, what is it?

DAVID

The British occupy the building where this guy, Hinkel, ran the Nazi Ministry of Culture and it seems they've – they've discovered his secret archive.

STEVE

What's that mean?

DAVID

I don't know, but the British are excited about it, I know that. The rumour is Hinkel kept a file on every artist working in the Third Reich.

STEVE

Jeez. And you think the British'll share it with their Allies?

DAVID

Major Richards said he'd call to let us know.

STEVE

That's big of him.

He looks from David to Emmi as if trying to work out something. Then:

STEVE

Okay, better question the next witness. I bet you a bottle of French champagne he tells us the baton story inside ten minutes.

DAVID

Five minutes.

STEVE

It's a bet. You're the witness, Emmi.

Later.

Rode in the witness chair. Steve studying the file. David and Emmi ready to take notes.

STEVE

Helmuth Alfred Rode. Second violinist since 1935. What's it mean, second violinist?

RODE

It means I wasn't good enough to be a first violinist.

He chuckles, looks around for approval. Steve grins encouragingly.

STEVE

Good, and according to your questionnaire, Helmuth, you never joined the Nazi Party.

RODE

Me? Never. Never.

Long silence.

I – I know everyone now says they were never Nazis but in my case it is absolutely one hundred per cent true. I am a Catholic, it would have been totally against my conscience.

Silence.

Steve lights a cigarette; Rode eyes it hungrily.

Is it true you're going to interview Dr Furtwängler today?

STEVE

I'll ask the questions, Helmuth.

RODE

Excuse me. Did you know that he refused to give the Nazi salute when Hitler was present in the audience?

Steve flicks David a glance, waggles his finger like a baton.

The problem was how could he avoid giving the Devil's salute when Satan was actually sitting there. (*Modestly taps his chest with his thumb.*) And, I said, 'Dr Furtwängler, why not enter with the baton in your right hand? Hitler will be sitting in the front row. If you give the salute with the baton in your right hand it'll look like you're going to poke his eyes out.'

Chuckles. David mouths 'I win' to Steve.

He was – He was really grateful to me for that. After the concert, I – I stole that baton as a memento of a great act of courage. I still have it. I should have brought it to show you. I hope I'm not going too fast for you, Fräulein –

EMMI

Straube.

Steve and David exchange a brief look.

RODE

Straube. Any relation to Colonel Joachim Straube?

EMMI

My father.

RODE
(*standing*)

I am deeply honoured to be in your presence, Fräulein Straube. Your father was a true patriot, a man of God.

He crosses himself. Silence. David raises a discreet finger.

STEVE

You have a question for Helmuth, David?

DAVID

Yes. What was the orchestra's reaction when they asked you to play for Hitler's birthday?

RODE

Oh, we didn't play for his birthday, we played the evening before – it was the 19th of April not the 20th.

STEVE

Do you know Hans Hinkel?

RODE
(*alarmed*)

Do I know Hans Hinkel?

STEVE

That's what I asked.

RODE

Do I know Hans Hinkel?

STEVE

You seem to understand the question, now how about answering it?

RODE

Hans Hinkel was in the Ministry of Culture; how could I know such a man?

Brief silence; a smile.

I hear the British have his – his archive, files, records.

STEVE

Do you know what's in this archive?

RODE

How could I know what's in the archive?

Steve nods, smiles.

STEVE

Okay, you can go now, Helmuth. Get out.

Rode stands and bows.

INT. STEVE'S OFFICE – NIGHT

The final bars of the Fifth Symphony. Snowing. Dim light. There is more furniture now: two chairs, one comfortable, the other upright. A sitting area by the window with the telephone extension. The 16-mm projector set up in another corner.

Steve, at his desk, wrapped up against the cold, going through files, making notes. He stops, seems to listen, then goes to the window, looks out.

The music ends. The record hisses. Steve just stares out at the night and the snow. The record continues to hiss.

INT./EXT TRAM, BERLIN (TRAVELLING) — DAY

The tram packed to overflowing. Then, a sudden stir among the passengers as people push through trying to find space. One of them is Furtwängler. He's recognised. Whispering. He stares ahead or keeps his eyes downcast. An elderly man tugs at his coat, half-rises, offering his seat. Furtwängler manages a smile and shakes his head. The tram rattles on.

INT. HALL, STEVE'S BUILDING — DAY

Furtwängler approaches Adams at his desk.

He crosses to the stairs. German workmen stop what they are doing to let him pass. One of them bows.

On the upper landing, Emmi is making her way to Steve's office.

She stops, sees Furtwängler on the stairs and then dashes to Steve's door.

FURTWÄNGLER
Furtwängler.

INT. STEVE'S OFFICE — DAY

Emmi bursts in on Steve and David. She's overawed:

EMMI
Major, Major – he's here . . .

STEVE
Shut the door, Emmi. Sit down, Emmi. We're going to keep him waiting, too.

Emmi glances out again and reluctantly closes the door. Steve sits calmly, relaxed.

> STEVE
>
> Emmi, get us some coffee, will you? And, Emmi, don't offer him coffee. Don't even greet him, okay?

INT. WAITING ROOM — DAY

Furtwängler sits, waiting. Emmi, deeply embarrassed, hurries through. Furtwängler is about to ask her something, but she's gone. He waits.

INT. STEVE'S OFFICE — DAY

Steve and David preparing papers.

INT. WAITING ROOM — DAY

Furtwängler waiting. Emmi enters from the landing door carrying a tray and three mugs of coffee. She hurries towards the office door, eyes downcast.

> FURTWÄNGLER
>
> Fräulein –?

Emmi stops.

> How long am I to be kept waiting?

Emmi bites her lip and, without looking at him, disappears into the office. Furtwängler closes his eyes, breathes deeply.

He stands, goes to the window, looks out.

INT. STEVE'S OFFICE — DAY

Silence. Steve studying his notes. David watching him. Emmi staring forlornly into space.

> STEVE
>
> Okay, Emmi, go get him.

Emmi rises, opens the door, nods, turns back to Steve.

Dr Furtwängler.

Furtwängler enters. As he passes her, Emmi gives him a small curtsey. David nods. Steve doesn't look up. Furtwängler waits a moment, glances round, sees the more comfortable chair and sits in it. Steve looks up.

STEVE

I didn't hear anyone invite you to sit down.

Furtwängler stands. Steve points to the other chair.

Sit there.

Furtwängler sits.

I want you to understand why you're here. You're automatically banned from public life under Control Council Directive No 24. We're here to look into your case before you appear in front of the Tribunal for Artists of the Denazification Commission. You understand that?

FURTWÄNGLER

I have already been cleared by a Denazification Tribunal in Austria.

STEVE

What they do in Austria doesn't interest me one little bit. Okay? I have your questionnaire here. (*reading*) Gustav Heinrich Ernst Martin Wilhelm Furtwängler, born Berlin, January 1886. Orchestral conductor. And you say here you were never a member of the Nazi Party.

FURTWÄNGLER

That is correct.

A very long silence. When the silence is unbearable Steve speaks.

STEVE

Could you tell us about being made a Prussian Privy Councillor. How did that happen to a non-Party member?

FURTWÄNGLER

I received a telegram from Hermann Goering informing me that he had made me a Privy Councillor. I was not given the opportunity either to accept or refuse. After the dreadful events of November 1938, the violent attacks on the Jews, I stopped using the title.

STEVE

What about Vice-President of the Chamber of Music, you used that title didn't you? But then I suppose you had no choice there either, because I suppose Dr Goebbels just sent you a telegram saying, Dear Mr Vice-President.

FURTWÄNGLER

I don't think Dr Goebbels sent me a telegram. I was simply told. In a letter, I believe. I don't remember exactly.

STEVE

Goebbels and Goering were sure heaping honours on you. One makes you a Privy Councillor, the other makes you Vice-President of the Chamber of Music, and you weren't even a member of the Party, how do you explain that?

FURTWÄNGLER

Well, there was a constant battle between Goering and Goebbels as to which of them would control German culture. I was simply a pawn. Anyway, I resigned from the Musikkammer at the same time I resigned as Musical Director of the Berlin Philharmonic Orchestra. In 1934.

David puts up a hand. Steve nods.

DAVID

Why was that? Why did you resign, Dr Furtwängler?

FURTWÄNGLER

I wrote an open letter to the newspapers condemning what they were doing to music, making these distinctions between Jews and non-Jews. For my part, the only divide in art is between good and bad. Eventually, Goebbels summoned me and told me I could leave the country if I wanted to but under no condition would I ever be allowed to return. I always believe that you have to fight from the inside not from without. I asked myself, what's the duty of an artist, to stay or to leave? And then Goebbels demanded that I acknowledge Hitler as solely responsible for cultural policy. Well, that was a fact and it seemed pointless to deny it. I simply acknowledged that Hitler and the Minister of Culture appointed by him were solely responsible for the cultural policy of the Reich. What I wanted to express was that I, personally, had no responsibility whatsoever for their cultural policy. I have always had the view that art and politics should – should have nothing to do with each other.

STEVE

Then why did you conduct at one of their Nuremberg rallies?

FURTWÄNGLER
(*flaring*)

I did not conduct at at the rally, I conducted on the evening before the rally –

STEVE

That sounds like the small print in one of our insurance policies, Wilhelm. And what about April 19, 1942? The eve of Hitler's fifty-third birthday, the big celebration; you conducted for Hitler, didn't you? Was that in keeping with your view that art and politics have nothing to do with each other?

FURTWÄNGLER
(*flustered*)

That – that was a different matter, I – I was tricked –

STEVE

How come?

FURTWÄNGLER

Could I have a glass of water, please? Please, Fräulein?

EMMI

Straube.

Steve looks expectant but Furtwängler remains silent. Steve nods to Emmi, who gets the water. Furtwängler drinks. Steve waits.

FURTWÄNGLER

Thank you. I was in Vienna, rehearsing the Ninth Symphony
of Beethoven, when Goebbels called and said I had to
conduct at Hitler's birthday. I'd always managed to wriggle
out of such invitations, pleading previous engagements,
illness, having my doctors state I was not well and so on
and so on. I was also fortunate that Baldur von Shirach,
who controlled Vienna, hated Dr Goebbels and would do
anything to thwart his wishes. But this time Goebbels got
to my doctors before me; they were frightened off, and von
Schirach was threatened, bullied and gave in. So, I had no
alternative but to conduct for Hitler. Believe me, I knew
I had compromised, and I deeply regret it.

STEVE
(*playing with him*)

Doesn't sound much of a trick to me. Sounds like you made
a deal –

FURTWÄNGLER

I made no deal –

STEVE

I don't buy that –

FURTWÄNGLER

It's the truth.

Silence. Steve paces. Then suddenly turns on Furtwängler.

STEVE

I keep hearing you helped a lot of Jews to escape. How did
you do that?

FURTWÄNGLER

I don't remember in detail, there were so many.

STEVE

Did you call someone you knew?

FURTWÄNGLER

I may have, as . . . as I said, I simply don't remember.

STEVE

Let me me help you, then. You picked up the phone and
made a call – (*Mimes a telephone.*) 'Hello, Adolf? Wilhelm
speaking. Listen, old pal, there's a Jew-boy musician I want
you to help. He needs a permit to get to Paris.'

Emmi sticks her fingers in her ears and shuts her eyes tight.

Or maybe you called Goebbels or Goering? You were so
close you were in the same shithouse as them.

FURTWÄNGLER

May I ask a question?

STEVE

Sure.

FURTWÄNGLER

When will my case be heard by the Tribunal?

STEVE

Your guess is as good as mine.

FURTWÄNGLER

I need to work. I need to make my living. I live off the
generosity of friends –

STEVE

Tough, tough –

FURTWÄNGLER
(*now more and more agitated*)

Then why is it, please, that another conductor who was
actually a member of the Party, who used to play the Horst
Wessel before his concerts, has already been cleared and is
working again while I have to wait and wait and wait?

STEVE

I don't know – he wasn't my case. Why did you escape to
Switzerland just before the war ended?

FURTWÄNGLER

It was because I learned that the Gestapo was about to
arrest me.

STEVE

Why were they going to arrest you?

FURTWÄNGLER

I believe it was because of another letter I'd written to Goebbels lamenting the decline of musical standards due to racial policies.

STEVE

You didn't complain about the racial policies, just about the musical standards, is that right?

No response.

So, how did you learn that the Gestapo was out to get you?

FURTWÄNGLER

During an enforced hour-long interval because of a power failure at a concert here in Berlin, Albert Speer, the Minister of Armaments, said to me, 'You look very tired Dr Furtwängler, you should go abroad for a while.' I knew exactly what he meant.

STEVE

You sure knew a lot of people in high places.

FURTWÄNGLER

It would be truer to say, I think, that a lot of people in high places knew me.

STEVE

You were real close to all of them, to Adolf, to Hermann, to Joseph, to Baldur, and now Albert. (*flaring*) So, let's hear the truth, let's come clean. What was your Party number?

FURTWÄNGLER

If you are going to bully me like this, Major, you had better do your homework. You obviously have no idea how impertinent and stupid your questions are.

Steve is stung. His eyes narrow dangerously.

STEVE

David, you remember I said I had a question that he wouldn't be able to answer? Well, I'm gonna ask it now. You

ready for this, Wilhelm? It's a tough one. Why didn't you
get out right at the start when Hitler came to power in 1933?
Why didn't you leave Germany?

No response.

I have a list of names here, people in your profession, who
got out in '33. Bruno Walter, Otto Klemperer, Arnold
Schoenberg, Max Reinhardt –

FURTWÄNGLER
They were Jews, they had to leave. They were right to leave.
(*He breathes deeply, summons strength.*) I could not leave
my country in her deepest misery. After all, I am a German.
I – I stayed in my homeland. Is that my sin in your eyes?

STEVE
See, David? He can't answer the question. I'll ask it again,
Wilhelm, and don't give me any more airy-fairy, intellectual
bullshit –

The telephone rings. No one moves. Then Emmi picks up the telephone.

EMMI
Major Arnold's office. Yes, he is.

Offers the phone to David.

It's Major Richards for Lieutenant Wills.

David takes the telephone.

DAVID
David Wills. Yes, sir. (*Listens.*) Well, you want me to tell him?
Okay. (*to Steve*) Major Richards wants a word with you, sir.

Steve indicates he'll take the call on the extension.

Furtwängler stands. As Steve crosses to the extension:

STEVE
(*muttering*)
Why can't he just ask for me? Why does he have to ask for
you first? Goddamn British, so correct –

He picks up the extension. Emmi puts down her receiver.

Steve Arnold –

FURTWÄNGLER
FURTWÄNGLER
I've had enough of this, I'm leaving.

He goes quickly. David dashes after him.

INT. WAITING ROOM — DAY

Furtwängler is at the door when David reaches him.

DAVID
Dr Furtwängler! Dr Furtwängler! Please, please – (*a
warning*) Don't. It's not advisable.

The sound of Steve laughing with delight. Furtwängler hesitates.

Emmi comes to the waiting-room door, watches, as if on guard.

David comes round to face Furtwängler.

DAVID
(*he gathers courage*)
When I was a child, my father, he took me to – he took
me to one of your concerts. I remember you conducted
Beethoven's Fifth Symphony. I was deeply moved. And
I've loved music ever since. I was grateful to you. And I've
admired you. How could you – how could you serve those
criminals?

He falls silent.

INT. STEVE'S OFFICE — DAY

*Emmi, at the open door, has been listening. She's shocked, turns away
to see Steve, on the extension, chuckling, grinning from ear to ear.*

STEVE
How many? Jesus, that's dynamite!

STEVE
Okay.

INT. WAITING ROOM — DAY

David and Furtwängler haven't moved. Both are looking towards Steve's office and Emmi in the doorway.

Again the sound of Steve's laugh. Then Emmi steps into the room, approaches Furtwängler.

EMMI

Dr Furtwängler –

He gives her a wonderful smile.

And, suddenly, Steve stands in the doorway, smiling.

STEVE

Well now. Aren't we all sociable?

The others are made awkward.

I've got to hand it to the British, David. You know what those guys are? Decent. (*He sits, crosses his legs.*) Tell me, Herr Dr Furtwängler, do you know Hans Hinkel?

FURTWÄNGLER

Yes, a despicable a human being. He was in the Ministry of Culture. His job was to get rid of Jews in the arts.

STEVE

Yup, that's him, that's the guy. You know what else the little creep did? He kept files, close on 250,000 files. And you know what's in those files?

FURTWÄNGLER

Certainly not, but I knew he had informers everywhere. Even in my orchestra there was someone

STEVE

Who?

FURTWÄNGLER

I wasn't told. I just knew it.

STEVE

How?

FURTWÄNGLER
(*uneasy*)

I was warned.

STEVE

Who warned you?

FURTWÄNGLER
(*lowering his head*)

Goering. Because Hinkel was working for Goebbels.

STEVE

What did Goering say?

FURTWÄNGLER

He told me to be careful as one of Goebbels' men was
watching me. He read a report on me – everything I said
was quoted word by word.

STEVE

Oh boy, you're gonna love this. Take your time with this
now. Those files contain the details of every working artist
in this country. Those files are gonna tell us who joined the
Party, who informed and who was helpful.

*Furtwängler goes to the door. David opens it for him. Furtwängler
nods, then turns to Emmi, bows to her and smiles. He goes.*

INT. BRITISH INTELLIGENCE HQ, ARCHIVE ROOM – DAY

SECURITY

Your name, please.

DAVID

David Wills.

SECURITY

Over there.

*There is a long trestle table running the length of the room, with
chairs, as if in a library. A notice requests 'Silence'.*

*British and American servicemen, a Russian and a French officer
studying papers, making notes. At the furthest end, Steve, David and
Emmi.*

STEVE

Fantastic! The only condition is we have to do the work
here. I want you to collect all the files on the boys in the
band.

INT. BRITISH INTELLIGENCE HQ, ARCHIVE ROOM — NIGHT

*David discovers that the archive room was originally a synagogue.
He is moved. He lays stones on the rail of what was once the ark.*

INT. BRITISH INTELLIGENCE HQ, ARCHIVE ROOM — DAY

Emmi and David surrounded by files, sifting through, making notes.

They examine the Hinkel Archive.

INT. BRITISH INTELLIGENCE HQ, ARCHIVE ROOM — DAY

Another day.

*Sunshine pouring in. Steve seated as before, but Emmi and David
again in different places.*

Emmi rises, goes to Steve, shows him something.

EMMI

Maybe you can have a look at this.

*He reads. He is not pleased. He writes furiously. Emmi returns to her
place. Suddenly, a movement causes Steve to look up.*

Steve and his point of view:

*David slides a note across to Emmi. Emmi reads the note. David
watches her. She looks at him. She almost smiles, nods surreptitiously.*

DAVID
(*a whisper*)

Schubert.

She feels Steve's eyes on her, and returns quickly to her work.

Steve is displeased and even more suspicious.

EXT. PARTLY RUINED CHURCH — EVENING

Summer evening. The first movement of Schubert's String Quintet in C Major, D956, played by three men and two women to a large audience packed into the ruins, partly open to the sky, Dymshitz among them.

At the rear of the church, Emmi and David, enraptured, seated side by side.

The first movement ends and the Adagio begins. After the music gathers momentum:

Rain. Thunder and lightning. The musicians continue to play, unperturbed. They are coming to the end of the Quintet.

David and Emmi huddled together. Some umbrellas up and then movement which catches David's attention. He nudges Emmi, indicates with his chin.

People have moved to reveal Furtwängler: seated, wearing a hat, still as a statue, soaked, listening, expressionless.

Much applause. The musicians bow. The audience start to leave.

Emmi and David emerge from the ruins. Furtwängler passes them.

They nod awkwardly. He doesn't respond but is about to walk on when Dymshitz pushes through, nods to David, who salutes. Dymshitz catches up with Furtwängler. They are near to Emmi and David.

DYMSHITZ

Dr Furtwängler –

Furtwängler stops.

Moving, you agree? Whenever I hear Schubert I am moved. You agree?

FURTWÄNGLER

The tempi were a little too correct for my taste. But I expect that is because of the rain.

He nods politely, is about to go –

DYMSHITZ
(*also for David's benefit*)
Wait, Doctor, I understand you have difficulties with the Americans. I want you to know, I am your champion. We can help.

Furtwängler allows himself a faint smile, tips his hat, and then hurries off into the night. Dymshitz goes, too.

David and Emmi watch them. Then:

EMMI
(*frowning, worried*)
What does he mean, too correct?

DAVID
I don't know.

Huddled under their umbrella, they dash off.

INT. STEVE'S BEDROOM, GRAND HOTEL — NIGHT

Steve, fully dressed, lies on the bed in his small, shabby room, staring into space. He is suddenly startled by a loud roll of thunder and then a fierce crack of lightning.

He goes to the window, watching the rain. He stands motionless for a second, then makes a decision. He grabs his cap, a raincoat from the back of the door. Another loud thunderclap.

INT. US OFFICERS' CLUB — NIGHT

Dancers jitterbugging and jiving. Among them, David and Emmi also dancing, imitating the others and having a good time. The music ends. Scattered applause. The band leaves the platform. The dancers return to tables or the bar.

Later:

David and Emmi at their table, eating. She eats voraciously, eyes glazed, all her concentration on the food in front of her. David is fascinated, can't stop watching her.

Steve enters the club, makes his way to the bar, orders a drink.

Steve turns to survey the room, almost at once spots David and Emmi, their backs to him. He observes them.

David and Emmi at their table:

They have finished their meal. Emmi is silent now, staring at her empty plate.

Steve is suddenly at their table.

STEVE

Well, what is this, the office party?

David and Emmi are frozen with embarrassment.

May I join you? (*Sits down, beams.*) So, what have you two been up to tonight? Hey. Don't I owe you a bottle of French champagne?

Tries to get a waiter's attention but fails.

No response.

You know, David, you're a lucky guy. I invited Emmi here but she turned me down. You must've hidden depths, David –

The band starts to play; he stands, holds out a hand.

C'mon, Emmi, let's dance. I'll teach you how to jive –

She is horribly embarrassed, doesn't move. David suddenly stands and takes Emmi by the arm.

DAVID

I'm very sorry, Major, but I promised her mother, we have to go.

They leave quickly. Steve watches them. He sinks down, angry and jealous.

INT. HALL, STAIRWAY, STRAUBE APARTMENT BLOCK – NIGHT

David and Emmi enter the hall, each locked in their own thoughts. They reach the foot of the stairs and pause. They want to kiss but both are too awkward. She starts up the stairs.

EMMI

Don't see me to my door, there's no need.

DAVID

But I promised your mother –

She stops, turns.

EMMI

Well, sleep well.

She continues on her way.

INT. ARCHIVE ROOM — DAY

Steve and Emmi at work on the files. One or two British officers present, and David, who is working at the far end of the table. He has a cold.

Emmi, who also has a cold, opens a file and is immediately alert. She reads. She blows her nose. She is uncertain. She looks up at Steve. She makes a decision. She rises, takes the file to Steve.

EMMI

Excuse me, Major. I found this on Helmuth Rode. You remember? The second violinist? Look, he's Austrian not German. But it's this that's more important, I think –

She points to something. Steve laughs loudly.

AN OFFICER

Sssh!

David looks up at them, puzzled. Then a British Sergeant comes into the doorway.

SERGEANT

Lieutenant Wills, telephone –

David rises and as he goes:

THE OFFICER
(*exasperated*)

What is this, a railway station?

INT. LOBBY, ARCHIVE BUILDING — DAY

In a booth near the front desk, David is on the telephone.

> DAVID
> (*into telephone*)
> David. Wills. Hello? Who? Who in Wiesbaden?

Irritated, he taps the receiver but the line's gone dead.

EXT. LAKESIDE, BERLIN — DAY

Steve lies, shirt off, taking the sun. Children playing. Noise behind him of someone in the bushes. Steve doesn't move.

Rode, carrying a slender leather case, pushes through to Steve, who remains with his eyes closed.

> RODE
> Major —

> STEVE
> (*eyes still closed*)
> Helmuth.

> RODE
> Guess what I am holding in my hand. You like guessing games?

> STEVE
> Love 'em, Helmuth. I give up. What are you holding in your hand?

Rode takes from the case a conductor's baton. Steve opens one eye.

> RODE
> It's Dr Furtwängler's baton, which I stole.

> STEVE
> The one he kept in his right hand.

> RODE
> Yes, you remember.

STEVE

How could I forget?

Sits up, takes the baton. Somewhere a child laughs; suddenly Steve thrusts the baton at Rode.

Show me.

RODE

Show you?

STEVE

Yeah, show me, I want to see you do it. Pretend I'm Adolf. You're the maestro, and you have the baton in your right hand, but you give me the salute just the same.

RODE

Not here, Major, there are people, if anybody should see – please, please, Major –

STEVE

Do it, Helmuth.

After nervous looks over his shoulder Rode, salutes half-heartedly.

Do it right.

Rode thrusts his hand out in the Nazi salute.

People by the lake:

Mostly elderly, but some younger ones see Rode saluting. Some turn away. Others stare.

STEVE'S VOICE

You look great doing that –

Rode and Steve:

Rode looks around nervously, lowers his arm.

STEVE

And I see what you mean. You nearly poked my eyes out.

RODE

Exactly.

Replaces the baton, gives Steve the case.

> STEVE
>
> Don't worry, Helmuth, it'll be our secret.

A ball comes bounding towards them. Steve catches it. Then a boy runs in, looks hopeful.

> BOY
>
> Mister, mister, here, here, mister!!!

Steve tosses the ball back to him.

> STEVE
>
> Great catch, kid.

The boy runs off.

> RODE
>
> So. You wanted to see me.

Steve pats the spot next to him and Rode sits.

> You usually don't work on Sunday, Major –

> STEVE
>
> All in the cause of humanity, Helmuth. Or should I call you one–zero–four–nine–three–three–one?

> RODE
>
> What?

> STEVE .
>
> One–zero–four–nine–three–three–one. Or d'you mind if I just call you 'one'?

Rode makes an attempt to go but Steve grabs him.

> You know what I say you are, Helmuth? I say you're a piece of shit.

Rode suddenly starts to retch.

> RODE
>
> That bastard –

People by the lakeside:

Faces turning at Rode's sobs. Impassive. Blank.

Steve and Rode:

> STEVE
> Who's the bastard, Helmuth? Hinkel?

Rode nods.

> Why? He promised to remove your file?

Rode vomits.

> And what about before that? What were you a member of in Austria −?

After a moment:

> RODE
> (*barely audible*)
> I was a member of −

> STEVE
> Speak up −

> RODE
> I was a member of the Communist Party. I was a communist. That's what Hinkel had over me. He knew everything. He held that over me. That's how he made me co-operate −

> STEVE
> Oh, I see, he made you co-operate. And now are you a communist again?

> RODE
> (*angry*)
> You don't know what it's like to wake up every single morning of your life terrified, you don't know that − (*He stops.*)

Brief silence. Steve stands.

Further along the lakeside:

Steve and Rode walk. People about. Boats on the lake.

RODE

I would never, in my wildest dreams, have ever been a second violinist in the Berlin Philharmonic. When they got rid of the – the Jews in the orchestra, it gave people like me a chance.

EXT. LAKE – DAY

Rode rowing Steve in a small boat. Rode, exhausted, stops. The boat drifts. Steve watches him for a moment, then:

STEVE

Helmuth, you ever heard of plea-bargaining?

Rode, trying to catch his breath, shakes his head.

Talk about power, I have the power to give you work, make your life easier. Your past won't be mentioned. I could give you a job tomorrow but I have to get something in return. See, Helmuth? That's plea-bargaining.

No response. Rode keeps his head bowed.

I can give you freedom of movement, freedom to work, freedom, Helmuth. But I need something in return.

RODE

Major, we're discussing a man of genius, I don't want –

STEVE

Fuck that, Helmuth. You want to discuss symbols here? This guy was a front man. He was the piper, but he played their tune, you get my philosophical meaning? I'm not interested in small fish, I'm after Moby Dick. Come on, Helmuth. Hard facts.

Silence. Then Rode slowly raises his head.

RODE

The only thing I know is he's an anti-Semite.

STEVE

Of course. You, too. Like everyone else in this goddamn country.

EXT. WOOD, LAKESIDE — DAY

Rode and Steve walking.

Rode suddenly turns to him:

> RODE
>
> I've remembered something else –

> STEVE
>
> Yeah?

> RODE
>
> Furtwängler sent Hitler a telegram for his birthday.

> STEVE
>
> He did?

> RODE
>
> One of your people told me –

> STEVE
>
> One of my people?

They start to walk away from the water.

> RODE
>
> Yes. A corporal. US Army. A Jew. He said he'd seen the telegram in the Chancellery.

> STEVE
>
> Son-of-a-gun. We'll find the corporal and we'll find the telegram.

He stops, takes out a cigarette, offers one to Rode, lights them both, gives Rode the packet.

They smoke for a moment.

> STEVE
>
> But I need documentary proof. You know of anything like that?

> RODE
>
> No. But that's why we hated him. We admired him as a conductor but we all hated him too because he didn't have

to join the Party and yet he had a better life than any of us. He didn't have to go and deliver a report after every trip abroad. He got everything from them, everything. He was filthier than any of us Party members.

The sun is setting. Rode stops suddenly.

RODE

There's a rumour – I don't know if it's true or not – but ask him about von der Nüll.

STEVE

Never heard of him, who is he?

RODE

Edwin von der Nüll. Music critic. He gave Furtwängler terrible reviews while he raved about Herbert von Karajan.

STEVE

Who's he?

RODE

Also a conductor. Very brilliant. Young. Von der Nüll called him 'The Miracle von Karajan'. Furtwängler was outraged and they say he had von der Nüll conscripted into the army. The same thing happened to another critic. True or not, it's not such a bad idea. Critics give you bad reviews, you have them sent to the Russian front. (*Chuckles.*) But if you really want to get Furtwängler, ask him about Herbert von Karajan.

STEVE

The Miracle Kid.

RODE

Yes, yes you may notice that he cannot even bring himself to utter his name, he – he refers to him as K.

Rode tries to make up his mind about something, then decides. He reaches into an inside pocket and takes out a small black notebook.

And ask him about his private life.

His private life?

Rode hesitates, then he hands Steve the black book.

RODE
Yes, it's all in here. His women –

INT. ARCHIVE ROOM – DAY

Steve going along the shelves filled with files. He's at the H, then I, then J. He stops at the letter K. With his forefinger, he runs down the files. He stops, pulls out a fat file:

'KARAJAN, H. VON'

He opens the file.

Insert – the file:

ID photographs of an energetic-looking young man and two Nazi Party membership booklets.

INT. CAFETERIA – DAY

David makes his way from the counter. He carries a tray with two cups of coffee. He goes to a table where Captain Martin sits, papers and files spread before him. David gives him his coffee, then sits across from him, blows his nose.

Silence while they sugar and milk their coffee. David aware of Martin's eyes on him.

MARTIN
Where do you stand on all this?

DAVID
On all what?

MARTIN
On Furtwängler.

DAVID
I don't know.

He breaks off.

MARTIN

You represent the United States now. We have a moral duty
to be just and we have to be seen to be just –

DAVID

Major Arnold believes he has a moral duty, too –

MARTIN

Our duty is to help Furtwängler with his defence. (*carefully*)
That's why I want you to look at this – (*He selects papers
from the table.*) These are part of the transcripts of the trial
at Nuremberg. We can't get them translated fast enough.
But I guess you understand German, right?

Passes papers across to David.

That's the evidence of a guy named Dahlerus. He's a
Swede. Friend of Hermann Goering. I want you to study it.
And I want you to use it.

David tries to sneeze but fails; he starts to read.

We're going to find more stuff to feed you. We'll have some
other suggestions. We need to build a case for the defence –
based not on feelings, not on prejudice, but on facts.

*He watches David read. David is engrossed. Almost imperceptibly, he
shakes his head.*

EXT. BERLIN STREET – DAY

*A half-ruined café with tables on the sidewalk. Werner, the timpanist,
Schlee, the oboist, and two others seated at one of the tables, drinking
coffee.*

*David carries an attaché case and walks towards the café. He scans
the people at the tables, sees the musicians and approaches. They stand.*

WERNER

Lieutenant Wills.

David nods.

Herr Schlee, timpanist, Herr Römer, cello and Herr
Schmidt, viola. They are willing to help. We have already
ordered ourselves coffee. I hope you –

DAVID

Yeah, of course.

WERNER

The whole orchestra will vouch for him. He was always
there to support us.

DAVID

We need names, if possible with addresses, because it's
urgent. Names of musicians saved by Dr Furtwängler,
people he helped to escape abroad. Let's go somewhere less
public –

*David leaves money on the table and then walks off with the four
men. They talk as they make their way down a side street.*

INT. DYMSHITZ'S VILLA – NIGHT

*Steve and Dymshitz sit opposite each other and clink vodka glasses.
They have been drinking but are not yet drunk.*

DYMSHITZ

To co-operation.

They drink. Dymshitz pours more vodka.

STEVE

I was in Vienna. I had with me an Austrian chauffeur, Max
his name was, he spent time in the camps. We were looking
at these Viennese cleaning up the bomb damage, scavenging
for rotting food, butt ends, anything. I said, 'To think a
million of these people came out to welcome Adolf on the
day he entered the city, a million of 'em, and now look at
'em.' And Max said, 'Oh, not these people, Major. These
people were all at home hiding Jews in their attics.' You get
the point, Colonel? The point is they're all full of shit.

DYMSHITZ

Furtwängler's in a different category.

STEVE

We're dealing with degenerates here.

He is still for a moment, then grabs the bottle and pours himself a drink, downs it. Dymshitz watches him, then:

DYMSHITZ

Degenerates?

INT. ANOTHER ROOM, DYMSHITZ'S OFFICE SUITE – NIGHT

German modern paintings stacked untidily.

Dymshitz, carrying a vodka bottle and his glass, shows Steve the paintings. Steve, too, has a glass.

DYMSHITZ

A great artist will have great privileges in a Russian zone.

STEVE

That's why he didn't get the hell out of here when he had the chance! I put that to him, he couldn't answer. Why didn't he go and direct in America, like that Italian, Toscanini.

Dymshitz pours vodkas, raises his glass, drinks. So does Steve. Now, their moods swing with the drink.

Dymshitz drinks; then sits, sinks into his own world.

DYMSHITZ
(lost for a moment)

Perhaps – perhaps he believed he could at least try to preserve something important, things like an orchestra, a school. That's his country. Maybe he has an old mother who can't be left alone. Maybe he has brothers, sisters – you can't –

A forlorn look at Steve. His eyes are misty, he is visibly drunk.

STEVE
(*a wry smile*)

Colonel. He had no sisters, no brothers, only a lot of love
affairs.

DYMSHITZ

Anyway, Major, why should he leave his country, his
mother tongue, his family, his history, his past, his future,
just because now, suddenly, there is a dictatorship? Why?

STEVE

But what – before that turns rotten – what if they surround
the space with barbed wire, Colonel?

DYMSHITZ
(*suddenly exploding*)

Don't talk about things you know nothing about. He was in
a dictatorship –

STEVE
(*dismissive*)

Yeah, yeah, art and politics, yeah, yeah, I heard all about
that –

DYMSHITZ
(*angry*)

In a dictatorship, art belongs to the Party. If you want to be
a conductor, you have to have an orchestra. And you can
only get an orchestra if you have contact with the power.
All over the world you need the right contacts and you have
to make the right compromises.

STEVE

This is what I'm saying. He must have had Party contacts.

DYMSHITZ

There are good Party members who help, and there are
dirty non-Party members who inform on you. Of course,
they gave him privileges.

Pause.

And suddenly, Steve, suddenly you notice that they like you. They honour you, suddenly you are the director of the best museum in the world, for example.

STEVE

What museum?

DYMSHITZ

I'm sorry. Museum? Not . . . I said orchestra. Sorry. Believe me. (*another sudden change of mood to earnest, intimate*) Help me, Steve. You say you answer for someone from high up. I, too, have orders from high up. Very high up. We want Furtwängler. I'll give you in return the whole orchestra, four, five conductors. I need him, Steve.

STEVE

No can do.

DYMSHITZ

Let Furtwängler go. Please.

STEVE

I have a duty –

DYMSHITZ
(*flaring*)

Duty? I am sorry, duty? Duty fucking duty. Trouble is, you Americans want everybody to live like you. We liberated Berlin, Major Steve, not you. Our duty also is to bring back the best of German culture.

Dymshitz bursts out laughing.

Stung, Steve advances on him, almost as if he's about to attack him physically. He stops, sways a little, then, after a moment, drops down in a chair near to Dymshitz. They drink. Intimate:

STEVE

I'm gonna get that fucking bandleader, Colonel. No deal. No fucking deal.

DYMSHITZ

Then you're going to kill me.

INT. STEVE'S OFFICE — NIGHT

Drunk, Steve is clumsily, almost frantically, threading film into the 16-mm projector.

He switches off the lights then stumbles back to the projector, turns it on and directs its beam towards a blank square of wall.

It's an American military propaganda film.

ARCHIVES

You'll see ruins, you'll see flowers, you'll see some mighty pretty scenery, don't let it fool you. You are in enemy country. The Nazi party may be gone, but Nazi thinking, Nazi training and Nazi trickery remain. Somewhere in this Germany are two million ex-Nazi officials. Out of power but still in there and thinking, thinking about next time. Remember that only yesterday every business, every profession was part of Hitler's system. Practically every German was part of the Nazi network. They believed they were born to be masters. Don't argue with them. You are not being sent Germany as educators. You're a soldier on guard. You will observe their local laws, respect their costumes and religion and you will respect their property rights. You will not be friendly. You will be aloof, watchful and suspicious.

Steve, swaying slightly, watches, with the film continuing.

EXT. FLEA MARKET — DAY

Bright summer's day. Emmi pushing her way through the crowded market. She comes to the stall with gramophone records.

David is with her, staying behind a little so as not to disturb her.

She starts to look through the records, blowing her nose from time to time. Then she finds a box of records, opens it, is delighted. She bargains with the stallholder, and she hands over money.

She shows her purchase to David happily. They struggle on in the crowd. David suddenly stops. He has spotted a tandem. The bicycle with two seats is old and rusty but seems to be in working order. David steps up to it, touches it.

EXT. WOODLAND — DAY

Two persons, Emmi and David, riding the tandem. Emmi in the front, pedalling, David behind. The road going up into the hills is full of potholes. They change seats. David is in the front, Emmi at the back. Suddenly the road begins to descend. They change again, Emmi sits in the front, David at the back. They speed down the hill.

INT. BURNT-OUT DEPARTMENT STORE — DAY

The tandem, ridden by Emmi and David, rolls into a huge building, black and burnt out.

In the middle of the vast hall, surrounded by the staircase, there is a Christmas tree, almost burnt to cinder. Emmi and David stare at it, mesmerised.

> DAVID
> Yesterday I read that Furtwängler was asked to lead the New York Philharmonic back in '36, Toscanini suggested it. Had he accepted, he would have become the most celebrated conductor in America.

> EMMI
> When he made his decision, he couldn't have known everything. Especially not the way people like you do, who've returned from exile and feel that you have a right to pass judgement. Because you are blameless, you think you know best who is a sinner and who deserves forgiveness. But you have no idea how people lived here.

> DAVID
> When he met Hitler at his birthday and shook hands with him, was he pleased?

> EMMI
> I don't know. But you and I already know that he has saved lives.

INT. STEVE'S OFFICE — DAY

Steve and David studying files in silence. Furtwängler's baton is on Steve's desk. Steve drinks black coffee.

Emmi enters. Curt nods of greeting. She goes to her desk, then takes the Bruckner record to Steve. Steve looks at the record, then glances up at Emmi. He does his best to exclude David, who tries to hear what is said.

Emmi glances at David. She's embarrassed.

EMMI

Bruckner's Seventh, Major.

STEVE

Do you know where the Adagio begins?

EMMI

Of course.

STEVE

Put it on ready to play, and I'll tell you when to play it.

He returns to his desk. Emmi looks through the album for the appropriate record.

INT. STEVE'S OFFICE — DAY

Steve by the open window, looking at his wristwatch, smoking a cigarette. David and Emmi both watch him.

The door opens and Furtwängler bursts in.

FURTWÄNGLER

It is now nine o'clock precisely. I do not intend to be kept waiting again.

STEVE
(*dangerously calm*)

Don't talk to me like I was a second violinist. Go back into the waiting room. Miss Straube will come and get you when I am ready to see you.

Furtwängler goes out.

STEVE

Jesus God, who the hell does he think he is? Who the hell does he think he is?

David and Emmi gaze at him as he tries to regain control.

INT. WAITING ROOM — DAY

The door to the landing is open and Rode is there pretending to sweep. He looks in to see Furtwängler sitting, holding his handkerchief over his nose and mouth.

> RODE
> Would you perhaps like to have a glass of water, Herr Professor?

Furtwängler doesn't seem to hear. Rode hesitates, then continues to sweep.

INT. STEVE'S OFFICE — DAY

David and Emmi look at him, puzzled.

She goes to the door, opens it, nods. Rode quickly disappears. Furtwängler looks at Emmi.

> FURTWÄNGLER
> What is this man doing here?

Emmi doesn't answer. All eyes on the door. Furtwängler enters.

> STEVE
> Dr Furtwängler! Come in, come in, sit down.

Furtwängler, deeply suspicious, goes for the uncomfortable chair.

> No, no, take this one, it's more comfortable

He holds the other chair for Furtwängler, who sits.

> If it's too hot, open your tie.

> FURTWÄNGLER
> (*interrupting*)
> I wish to say something.

> STEVE
> Go ahead, be my guest.

Furtwängler takes from his pocket a piece of paper with notes. He blows his nose. The room is warming up. It will become like an airless court room, a pressure cooker.

FURTWÄNGLER

When I last saw you, I was unprepared. I did not know what to expect. In these past weeks, I have been thinking more carefully and making some notes. (*Glances at the notes.*) You have to understand who I am and what I am. I am a musician and I believe in music. I am an artist and I believe in art. Art in general, and music, in particular, has for me mystical powers which nurture man's spiritual needs. I must confess, however, to being extremely naive. I insisted for many years on the absolute separation of art and politics. My entire life was devoted to music because, and this is very important, because I thought that I could, through music, do something practical.

STEVE

And what was that?

FURTWÄNGLER

Maintain liberty, humanity and justice.

STEVE

Gee, that's a thing of beauty, honest to God, a real thing of beauty. I'm going to try to remember that. Liberty, humanity and justice. Beautiful. But you used the word 'naive'. Are you now saying you think you were wrong? That art and politics can't be separated?

FURTWÄNGLER

I believe art and politics should be separate, but that they weren't kept separate I learned to my cost.

STEVE

And when did you first learn that – when you sent the telegram? Was that the surrender signal, the waving of the white flag?

FURTWÄNGLER

What telegram?

178

STEVE

'Happy birthday, dear Adolf, love Wilhelm.' Or words to
that effect. That sounds to me like you were dropping on
your knees and saying, 'Okay, Adolf, you win. You're the
number one man. Have a swell party.'

FURTWÄNGLER

I have no idea what you're talking about.

STEVE

The birthday greetings you sent to your old pal, Adolf Hitler.

FURTWÄNGLER

I never sent him any birthday greetings or any other kind of
greetings.

STEVE

Think carefully, Wilhelm – maybe not in your own name,
but as Privy Councillor or Vice-President.

FURTWÄNGLER

I don't have to think carefully. This is utterly ridiculous.

*David and Emmi exchange the briefest of looks. David raises his
hand.*

STEVE

Yes, David?

DAVID

Why not show Dr Furtwängler the evidence. It may refresh
his memory?

FURTWÄNGLER

You won't find it because no such telegram exists.

STEVE

Well, I tried, you got to admit I tried. I thought I might just
trap you there, Wilhelm, but David here was too quick for
me. Smart move, David, smart move. No, I don't have the
telegram, but I know it exists. And I want you to know,
Wilhelm, we're going to keep looking for it because I believe
you sent it.

FURTWÄNGLER

Then you are wrong.

STEVE

Art and politics, yeah, art and politics. Let's look at that.
You and the Berlin Philharmonic toured the Third Reich,
played in countries the Nazis had conquered. Are you
saying that conducting in occupied territories from 1939
on wasn't a commercial for Adolf and all he stood for?

FURTWÄNGLER

We never, never officially represented the regime when we
played abroad. We always performed as a private ensemble.
As I think I already told you, I was a freelance conductor –

STEVE

You know something? You should've written our insurance
policies for us because you got more exclusion clauses than
Double Indemnity. What do you imagine people thought?
The Berlin Philharmonic's taken over by Doctor Goebbels
and his Propaganda Ministry but Wilhelm is a freelance, so
art and politics are now entirely separate? Is that what you
believed ordinary people thought?

FURTWÄNGLER

I have no idea what ordinary people thought –

STEVE

No –

FURTWÄNGLER

No, because I had only one intention. My only intention
whatever I did was to show that music means more than
politics.

STEVE

Tell me about von der Nüll.

FURTWÄNGLER
(taken off-guard)

Von der Nüll?

Yes, von der Nüll –

FURTWÄNGLER

Von der Nüll –

STEVE

How long's this going to go on, Wilhelm? I say von der
Nüll, you say von der Nüll, I say von der Nüll, you say von
der Nüll, we could go on all day. You know who von der
Nüll is, don't you? Edwin von der Nuell, music critic –

FURTWÄNGLER

Yes, I know who he is –

STEVE

Isn't it true that because he gave you bad reviews and
praised this young guy, Von Karajan, called him a goddamn
miracle, said he was a better conductor than you, then you
had von der Nüll conscripted into the army and no one's
heard from him since?

FURTWÄNGLER

That's an outrageous lie!

STEVE

You sure you didn't call one of your close buddies and say,
God in heaven, did you see what that guy von der Nüll
wrote about me? The greatest conductor on earth. I want
him out the way. He had the nerve to accuse me I am not
playing enough modern music. Send him to Stalingrad.
Isn't that what you did? You don't like criticism, do you,
Wilhelm? You surely didn't like them saying there was
another conductor who was better than you – Are you
saying the name von der Nüll was never mentioned in your
talks with Goebbels?

FURTWÄNGLER
(*uncomfortable*)

Well. Once he said he'd read what this man wrote about
me.

STEVE

And what did he say?

FURTWÄNGLER

He said, 'Don't mind him. His job is to criticise, your job is
to conduct.'

STEVE

And what happened to Von der Nül?

FURTWÄNGLER

I have no idea.

STEVE

You've really no idea? I'll tell you what happened. He died
in Stalingrad.

FURTWÄNGLER

I'm sorry.

STEVE

Now, that young conductor what's his name? (*playing with
Furtwängler*) That miracle kid, you know who I mean. Von
Karajan! But you called him something else. C'mon. What
did you call von Karajan?

Silence.

Say it.

Silence.

I'll say it, then. 'Little K.' Is that right? You couldn't even
bear to say his name –

Furtwängler rises angrily and starts to pace.

FURTWÄNGLER

Please stop playing these games with me. Why you should
bring up the name of another conductor is beyond my
understanding.

STEVE

I'll tell you why. You remember we talked about you playing
for Hitler's birthday? And you told me that Goebbels got to
your doctors first, that you were tricked?

FURTWÄNGLER

Yes, that's what happened –

He sits heavily, wipes his brow. He is sweating now.

STEVE

I have a different story to tell. I don't think you were tricked. Not in the way you describe. I believe something else happened. I've seen the Hinkel Archive, I've seen records of phone calls, and putting it all together, this is what I think happened. I think Goebbels said, 'Wilhelm, if you won't conduct for Adolf's birthday, we'll get the Miracle Kid, the guy that critic, von der Null, thinks is the greatest conductor in the world. He's not just willing to conduct for Adolf, he's offered to sing "Happy Birthday" as a solo.'

Silence.

Come on, admit it. K worried you, didn't he? He always worried you. In 1942, he's thirty-four years old, you're already fifty-six. And Goebbels and Goering keep saying to you, 'If you don't do it, little K will.' Never mind art and politics and symbols and airy-fairy bullshit about liberty, humanity and justice because I don't care how great you are. It's the oldest story in the book. (*a wry look at David*) The ageing Romeo jealous of the young buck. The real reason you didn't leave the country when you knew you should have was that you were frightened that, once you were out of the way, you'd be supplanted by the Miracle Kid, the Party's boy twice over, flashy, talented little K.

FURTWÄNGLER

This is absolute nonsense –

STEVE

Well, I'm just beginning to develop my theme. Isn't that what you call it in classical music, developing your theme? Okay, so they played on your insecurity. That's human, understandable. But, there is one guy who doesn't like little K as much as he likes you – yeah, the number one man your old pal, Adolf. He thinks you're the greatest, and when

183

he says, I want Wilhelm for my birthday, boy, they better go out get Wilhelm. So, Josef calls and threatens you with little K. And you said to hell with the Ninth in Vienna, I'll give it to Adolf as a birthday present in Berlin. That's the trick they played, they got you by the balls and they squeezed. Hard. Why did you stay? Why did you play for them? Why were you the flag-carrier for their regime? Jealousy –

FURTWÄNGLER
(*interrupting*)
Of course there was a conspiracy against me, a campaign – even abroad.

Brief silence; all eyes on him.

STEVE
You see, Wilhelm, I'm talking about ordinary, everyday reasons. Which is why I want to discuss your private life. How many illegitimate children do you have?

DAVID
Major, I don't see how this line of questioning could –

STEVE
David, what are you Counsel for the Defence now? (*to Furtwängler*) Did you hear the question?

FURTWÄNGLER
(*barely audible*)
I have illegitimate children.

STEVE
What?

FURTWÄNGLER
I said I have illegitimate children. I don't know how many –

STEVE
You like the women, don't you, Wilhelm?

No response.

Isn't it true that before every concert you got a woman in your dressing room and gave her the old conductor's baton, isn't that true –?

DAVID
(*indicating Emmi*)
Major, this is deeply offensive and repugnant –

STEVE
You bet –

DAVID
– and totally irrelevant.

STEVE
(*continuing to Furtwängler*)
Not so, Counsellor. That secretary of yours, she wasn't just your secretary, she procured women for you, didn't she? As many and as often as you wanted –

FURTWÄNGLER
Stop this, please, stop this now –

STEVE
No, I'm not going to stop it. Hitler himself offered you a beautiful house and a personal bomb shelter –

FURTWÄNGLER
I absolutely refused the house and the bomb shelter.

STEVE
But you see what I'm getting at? You get a gorgeous house, you're highly paid. What are you gonna do, stay or leave? One voice comes back at me: stay!

DAVID
Major, that's not a good argument. If Dr Furtwängler did indeed enjoy all these – these privileges, he enjoyed them because of who he is and what he is. That's true of any leading artist in any country in the world.

STEVE
But it still doesn't make them saints. They still have to get up and piss in the middle of the night, don't they? They can still be vindictive and envious and mean just like you and me. Well, just like me. Can't they?

No response. To Furtwängler:

Okay, Wilhelm, go home now. Go home and think about
these past twelve years.

FURTWÄNGLER

I don't understand what you mean.

STEVE

No, that's your problem, Wilhelm. You understand nothing.
We'll call you. Go!

Furtwängler leaves.

DAVID

Major.

Steve goes to his desk and, as Furtwängler rises uncertainly:

STEVE

What?

DAVID

Your manner –

STEVE

My manner? Why don't you go downstairs, get a cup of
coffee and calm down? What's the matter, Emmi? What's
going on with you? What's wrong?

EMMI

I'm sorry but I have to leave. I'll find other work. You'll
have to get someone else, that's all.

STEVE

What is this, Emmi?

EMMI

I can't do this. It's not right.

STEVE

What's not right?

EMMI

I have been questioned by the Gestapo just like that. Just
like you questioned him.

STEVE

Emmi, stop! I want to show you something. Let me show you something and then if you want to leave, you can leave, please please. His friends, they did this. And he gave them birthday concerts.

EMMI

But he had no idea, a lot of people had no idea. I only realised what was really going on when I got arrested.

STEVE

If he had no idea, why did the Jews need saving? This is my question, Emmi, to all Germans: Why did the Jews need saving in this country? Why, if people had no idea?

EMMI

I would like to go now, please.

But Steve turns on the projector and the Bergen-Belsen film flickers into life.

INT. US OFFICERS' CLUB — NIGHT

Band playing. Couples dancing. David and Steve at the bar, each with a drink in front of them, lost in their own thoughts. Then:

Steve signs to the barkeeper to fill their glasses but David puts a hand over his glass. Then:

DAVID

Can I ask you a favour, Major?

STEVE

Yeah –

DAVID

When you question him again, could you treat him with more respect?

STEVE

With more what? More what?

DAVID

Major, he may just be the greatest conductor of this century and that merits respect.

STEVE
(*flaring, hissing*)

David, I don't understand a thing about you. You're a Jew. Are you a Jew?

DAVID

Yes, I'm a Jew. But I like to think first I'm a human being.

STEVE

A human being, oh, good, I'm relieved, I thought you were going to say you were a music lover. This man, this great artist has made anti-Semitic remarks like you wouldn't believe. I got letters.

DAVID

Major, show me someone who hasn't made an anti-Semitic remark and I'll show you the gates of paradise.

STEVE
(*over-reacting and overlapping*)

What is it with you, David? Where are you feelings? Where's your hatred, your disgust? Where's your fucking outrage, David?

He starts to go, then comes back to them.

Think of your parents, David, and then think of him conducting 'Happy Birthday, dear Adolf'. I mean, for Chrissake, whose side are you on? Grow up! Just grow the fuck up!

The customers stare at him as he stalks out. The band plays.

Cut to:

INT. STRAUBE APARTMENT — EVENING

David and Emmi, sitting.

I want you to come back to the office. May I come in?
If you are there you can influence what happens. What
good can you do by leaving. If you go, you are giving up
and how can you help Furtwängler or me? Don't think
about leaving. Stay.

INT. STEVE'S OFFICE — DAY

*Hot. Windows closed. Furtwängler seated. David and Emmi present.
Steve looks up from his notes.*

STEVE

Everybody says what a great benefactor you were to the
Jews. But – (*Holds up a sheaf of papers.*) – I have things here
you said and wrote. Listen to this: 'The Jew composer
Schönberg is admired by the Jewish International.' And
what about this: 'Jewish musicians lack a genuine affinity
with our music.' 'Jewish musicians are good businessmen
with few scruples, lacking roots.' You deny you said these
things?

FURTWÄNGLER

Those attitudes do not exist in me.

STEVE

I believe that. But just answer the question, don't give me
explanations –

FURTWÄNGLER

Speaking to Party members I used their language, of course
I did, everyone did –

DAVID
(*with some irony*)

Major, sorry to interrupt, but maybe we have to – maybe
we have to balance those things against his assistance to his
Jewish colleagues.

Steve tenses.

This is a transcript of the proceedings at Nuremberg.
A Swedish businessman, Birger Dahlerus, testified in cross-

examination that he had several meetings with Hermann Goering. 'I first saw Goering,' Dahlerus testified, 'embroiled in a stormy interview with Wilhelm Furtwängler, the famous conductor of the Berlin Philharmonic, who was vainly seeking permission to keep his Jewish concert master.'

Holds up his package of letters and dumps them on Emmi's desk.

Emmi, pick one of these, any one, read it out loud.

Emmi is uncertain. Steve shrugs indifferently.

She picks an envelope and takes out the letter.

EMMI
(*reading*)

'Please remember that Dr Furtwängler risked his life to help anyone who asked him. I personally testify to having seen literally hundreds of people lined up outside his dressing room after concerts to ask for his help. He never turned anyone away. After he heard me play – I am a violinist – he gave me money because I was unable to feed myself or my family and then he helped me to escape to Sweden. He helped countless people in similar ways.'

DAVID

And this, only one of these letters, Major. I have lots of them.

STEVE
(*smiling*)

How many times have I got to tell you I was in insurance? You think I can't smell a phoney policy when it's shoved under my nose? Sure, he helped Jews, but that was just insurance, his cover, because all the while he was maestro of all he surveyed. (*turning on Furtwängler*) See, Wilhelm, I think you're their boy, their creature. You were like an advertising slogan for them: this is what we produce, the greatest conductor in the world. And you went along with it. The truth of the matter is, Wilhelm, you didn't need to be a member of the Party. I made a mistake when I asked you for your Party number. I should've asked you for your non-Party number. Just like some other well-known artists. (*suddenly, to Emmi*) Emmi, put that record on –

Emmi puts on the record of the Adagio from Bruckner's Seventh Symphony. After a moment:

Do you know what that is?

FURTWÄNGLER

Of course I know what that is –

STEVE

Okay, so what is it?

FURTWÄNGLER

Bruckner's Seventh. The Adagio.

STEVE

Who's conducting?

FURTWÄNGLER

I am.

STEVE

You know the last time it was played on these air waves?

FURTWÄNGLER

How can I know such a thing –?

STEVE

I'll tell you, then. The last time this music was played on these air waves was after they announced that your pal Hitler had shot himself. Listen to it.

They listen.

Did they pick little K's recording? Did they pick some other conductor? No, they picked you, and why? Because you represented them so beautifully. When the Devil died, they wanted his bandleader to conduct the funeral march. You were everything to them.

The music plays.

FURTWÄNGLER
(near to breakdown but struggling for control)

I have always tried to analyse myself carefully and closely. In staying here, I believed I walked a tightrope between exile and the gallows. You seem to be blaming me for not having allowed myself to be hanged.

David takes the record off.

I didn't directly oppose the Party because I told myself, that was not my job. If I had taken any active part in politics I could not have remained here. But as a musician, I am more than a citizen. I am a citizen of this country in that eternal sense to which the genius of great music testifies. I know that a single performance of a great masterpiece was a stronger and more vital negation of the spirit of Buchenwald and Auschwitz than words.

An uncontrollable surge of anger wells up in Steve, causing him to pace alarmingly. He grabs the baton from his desk, stands trembling before Furtwängler, and snaps it in half.

He pushes his face close to Furtwängler, who recoils, terrified. David half-stands, ready to intervene physically. During this Emmi puts her fingers in her ears.

STEVE
(quiet, terrifying)

Have you ever smelled burning flesh? I smelt it four miles away. Four miles away, I smelt it. Have you ever seen the gas chambers, the crematoria? Have you seen the mounds of rotting corpses? You talk to me about culture, art and music? You putting that in the scales, Wilhelm? You setting culture, art and music against the millions put to death by your pals? They had orchestras in the camps. They played Beethoven, Wagner. The hangmen were playing chamber music at home with their families. I don't understand the Germans' relationship with music. What do you need music for? Your pals you could call to save a few Jews when millions of them were being annihilated? Yes, I blame you for not getting hanged, I blame you for your cowardice. You strutted and swaggered, you fucking piece of shit, king-pin in a shithouse. You talk to me about walking a tightrope between exile and the gallows, and I say to you, lies –

FURTWÄNGLER
(*breaking down*)
I love my country, I believe in music, what was I to do?

STEVE
Look around you. See the country you served. Look at people who had real courage, who took risks, who risked their lives. Like Emmi's father.

He sees Emmi has her fingers in her ears, yells at her.

Emmi, take your fingers out of your ears –

She does so.

I'm talking about your father.

She screams. Stillness. All eyes on her.

EMMI
My father only joined the plot when he realised that we could not win the war.

She cries quietly.

FURTWÄNGLER
(*desperate*)
What kind of a world do you want, Major? What kind of world are you going to make? Do you honestly believe that the only reality is the material world, so you will be left nothing, nothing but feculence . . . more foul-smelling than that which pervades your nights –(*near to breakdown*) How was I to understand, how was I to know what they were capable of? No one knew. No one knew.

He breaks down, buries his face in his hands, weeps.

I don't want to stay in this country. Yes, I should have left in 1934, it would have been better if I'd left –

He is suddenly overtaken by nausea and faintness, stands, a hand to his mouth. Emmi goes to him.

STEVE

Get him out of here –

Emmi helps Furtwängler out. Steve strides to the window, opens it, puts his head out into the fresh air.

INT. WAITING ROOM – DAY

Emmi helps Furtwängler to a chair. She watches him solicitously. He breathes deeply.

FURTWÄNGLER

Thank you, Fräulein. You have been most kind. (*He rises.*)

He smiles at her. She is embarrassed.

INT. STEVE'S OFFICE – DAY

Steve is trying to get a number on the telephone. David is packing up his papers.

David turns to the records, starts to sort through until he finds what he's looking for. He removes the Bruckner and puts another record on the turntable.

STEVE
(*into the telephone*)

Major Arnold. Get me General Wallace. General? Major Arnold, about Furtwängler. I don't know if we've got a case that'll stand up, but sure as hell we can give him a hard time –

At full volume the sound of the subdued opening of Beethoven's Ninth Symphony.

STEVE
(*to David*)

Hey, turn that down, would you? Can't you see I'm on the phone? (*into the telephone*) Never mind, we got a journalist who'll do whatever we tell him.

But David ignores him, sits, implacable, listening.

INT. STEVE'S BUILDING — DAY

Furtwängler walks slowly down the stairs, a broken man struggling to regain his composure. Emmi watches him.

INT. STEVE'S OFFICE — DAY

The music at full blast. David, at an open window, keeps his back to Steve, still on the telephone.

STEVE
Turn it off!

EXT. STEVE'S BUILDING — DAY

Furtwängler, on the stairs, stops, hearing the music echoing through the building.

Furtwängler's left hand begins to tremble, but it is only his way of sensing the tempo.

Furtwängler slowly continues down the stairs.

STEVE'S VOICE
We handed Wilhelm Furtwängler over to the civil authorities and he was charged with serving the Nazi regime, with uttering anti-Semitic slurs, performing at an official Nazi Party function and with being a Prussian Privy Councillor. Dr Furtwängler was acquitted. I didn't nail him. But I sure winged him. And I know I did the right thing. Furtwängler resumed his career but he was never allowed to conduct in the United States. He died in 1954. Little K succeeded him as head of the Berlin Philharmonic.

INT. CONCERT HALL (ARCHIVE)

Furtwängler conducting. Goebbels and other high-ranking Nazis in the audience. When the music finishes, Furtwängler turns and bows. Goebbels rises and shakes hands with him. Furtwängler takes his handkerchief and wipes his hands. The film replays this gesture several times – Furtwängler wiping his hands.

Fade out.